THE

15

MINUTE INVESTOR

PROSPERITY AND PEACE OF MIND FOR THE PRICE OF A NEWSPAPER

CHET CURRIER AND THE ASSOCIATED PRESS

FRANKLIN WATTS
1986
NEW YORK/TORONTO

Library of Congress Cataloging in Publication Data
Currier, Chet.
The 15-minute investor.
Includes index.
1. Investment analysis.   2. Investments—United
States.   I. Associated Press.   II. Title.   III. Title:
Fifteen-minute investor.
HG4529.C87   1986   332.6'78   85-31752
ISBN 0-531-15502-1

CONTENTS

2275743

THE
15-MINUTE
INVESTOR

FOREWORD

ACKNOWLEDGMENTS

A 15-Minute Investor can be anyone who wants and needs to manage money effectively—in savings accounts, mutual funds, stocks, bonds, and other long-term investment vehicles—working with a limited amount of free time in a life filled with other responsibilities and interests.

The 15-Minute Investor is none of the following: a lifelong academic student of the securities markets; a sophisticated trader of futures, options, or currencies; an economist; or an expert of any kind. (The writer, it should be mentioned, is also none of those things.)

The goal of this book was to make the task of reading and understanding financial and economic news simple, without being simple-minded or overly simplistic. That proved to be no simple job.

In attempting it, the writer had the help and encouragement of many people, all of which was greatly appreciated. Special thanks go to Bill Newton, an editor who knows how to edit with or without a pencil in his hand; Dan Perkes; Mike Millican, and my colleagues in the Associated Press Business News Department; John Currier; Cathy and Fred Barberi, for their yeoman work in typing and transporting manuscript pages; and to Carol, Dana, and Craig Currier, who juggled work time, play time, even vacation time, so that this book could be written.

INTRODUCTION

INFORMATION, NEWS, AND THE STOCK MARKET

Many people have a strong desire to manage their savings and investments to the best possible advantage, and an active interest in the financial markets as well. But only a few are able and willing to follow events in the financial world minute by minute, every business day. In your job—computer programmer, dentist, teacher, salesperson, farmer, fulltime homemaker, or whatever—chances are your responsibilities keep you preoccupied with other matters while the stock market, interest rates, and many other forces that can affect your personal finances are constantly in motion. Even if you have no other commitments, you may have no desire to spend all your time keeping tabs on what's happening on Wall Street.

But it is also a fact of life that information, current information, is powerful ammunition in the battle for investment success. With it, you can hope to make your money work very hard for you. Without it, your chances are greatly diminished. That leaves you with a problem: How to keep yourself up-to-date on the state of the securities markets and the economy with a minimum investment of time. This book endeavors to provide a solution to that problem, using the daily or weekly business section of your newspaper to give your finances a regular checkup in about 15 minutes. It proposes a seven-step approach to gathering as much investment information and as many ideas as possible from the newspaper in that time.

The 15-Minute approach is no magic formula. It cannot put you in the same position as professional investors, who can watch the markets full time, and who use computers, financial news services, and other sophisticated (and expensive) means to uncover potential short-term opportunities. Rather, its purpose is to help you stay abreast of changing numbers and events while you pursue your long-term financial goals. The 15-Minute system is also intended to be flexible. If it suits your needs and temperament, you can follow it step-by-step as presented. If it doesn't, you can rework it to suit yourself.

Following the main section of this book are chapters on other sources of investment information with which you can supplement your regular 15-minute reviews, and on the language of Wall Street—so that when someone says something to you that sounds like impenetrable financial jargon, you can decide for yourself whether that person has some useful information to impart.

A STEP-BY-STEP GUIDE TO GIVING YOUR INVESTMENTS A REGULAR CHECKUP

CHAPTER ONE

NEWS ROUNDUP

As a 15-Minute Investor, your primary tool is your newspaper, be it a specialized publication such as the *Wall Street Journal,* or your local general-interest paper. You doubtless already are aware that the financial tables in the newspaper contain an enormous store of numbers, designed to tell you practically everything that takes place in public in the markets on any given business day.

For all practical purposes, you have neither the ability nor the desire to absorb all this information. The challenge, therefore, is to pick your way through the pages, harvesting the information of greatest importance to you, in about a quarter of an hour—over coffee in the morning, say, or in a favorite chair in the evening after the children have gone to bed.

Once settled down, undistracted, the 15-Minute Investor goes over the newspaper in this sequence:

1. *News Roundup.* Begin with a quick reading of the headlines on the front page, and on the main news page of the business section, for any political or economic developments that could affect your financial plans.

2. *Market Stories.* Once into the business section, read the roundup story or stories on the securities markets.

3. *Individual Investments.* Turning to the financial tables, consult individual listings of stocks, bonds, mutual funds, and any other investments you own or are considering for purchase.

4. *Market Statistics.* Review the tabular section listing the performance of the various indicators of the stock market, including stock-price averages and indexes, the most active list, and the lists of new highs and lows.

5. *Earnings Reports.* Check tables of quarterly corporate earnings and dividend reports for the latest basic financial information on any companies you are following.

6. *Economic Statistics, Analyses, and Investment Columns.* Go back over the stories in the business section, reading columns on investment subjects, economic analyses, and stories on any new statistical reports from the government.

7. *Freelancing.* After the first six prescribed steps, use whatever time remains to "freelance." Wander through the financial pages looking for anything that catches your attention, particularly among the shorter items that might appear at the bottom of a column on an inside page. Is there some new product, plant closing, or management change that warrants further investigation? If so, the news item might be clipped out and put in a convenient place for reference in that investigation.

In the pages that follow, we will discuss each of these steps in detail.

The first element in the regular routine of the 15-Minute Investor might seem patently obvious: checking the headlines on the front page and main business page for any item of interest. You don't need anyone to tell you how to do that.

But for beginning investors in particular, it takes some time and experience to learn to read the news from a financial point of view. Suppose, for example, you read that the latest government statistics show an increase in the birth rate in this country. The story may discuss the subject primarily as a social issue. But it poses other questions from an investment standpoint. For instance, does this raise the prospect of significant increases in sales for companies that make toys or baby food? If so, is it news that hasn't been widely recognized to date by other participants in the stock market?

Sometimes the process of sorting out the investment implications of a news item is pretty cold-blooded. Suppose a story tells of a disaster in which many lives have been lost and much property destroyed. For an investor, the questions that come to mind may seem very insensitive: What companies, if any, are involved? Will the disaster disrupt their operations or hurt their public image? Do they face potential lawsuits and damage claims, and are they covered by insurance?

A tale that has been told and retold on Wall Street concerns a veteran investor who reads of an epidemic of heroin abuse and its frightening impact on many individuals and on American society as a whole. Muses the investor: "I wonder who makes the needles." The story, extreme as it is, makes a point. Within the regulatory boundaries in which they operate, markets themselves are amoral and pitiless.

Does that mean that the 15-Minute Investor must become amoral and pitiless, too, in order to participate in the markets? Most definitely not. In fact, more and more individual investors—and institutions such as mutual funds—are operating these days from a social or ethical viewpoint, and claiming success on the bottom line from their endeavors. People who disapprove of liquor, for example, may rule out stocks of distilling companies from their investment plans.

Still, a detached point of view is an important asset in the quest for investment success. In suggesting that his customers might profit from an investment in tobacco stocks, veteran stockbroker Lucien Hooper once observed, "You don't have to endorse smoking to do it. You are only recognizing that bad habits usually are profitable for those who exploit them."

Evaluating the news from an investment perspective isn't always a grim business. A generation ago, when women were more inclined to follow rigid dictates of fashion than they are today, the "hemline indicator" evolved on Wall Street. Under this doctrine, prevailing skirt lengths provided a qualitative measure of the public mood. Long skirts signaled a time of somberness and caution, unconducive to any boom in the stock market. The

1960s, on the other hand, saw the arrival of both miniskirts and one of the most powerful bull markets in modern history.

The hemline indicator may be dated today, and it never was a sure, easy way to get rich in the stock market (there are no sure, easy ways). But in its time, it made more sense than a lot of other methods people were using to try to figure out where stocks and other investments were headed. It also served to illustrate that investment ideas can be found almost anywhere you choose to look.

CHAPTER TWO

MARKET
STORIES

Once having reviewed the general and business headlines of the day, the 15-Minute Investor turns to a standard item in most newspapers—the story covering the latest activity in the securities markets themselves. Some papers also carry a separate review of activity in the credit (bond and short-term money) markets, and perhaps of the currency and commodities markets as well. All these are worth at least a quick reading.

What information of value can you expect from these stories? The reporters who write them seek to summarize general trends in the market, working with much of the same information available to you—market indexes, the list of the most active stocks, biggest percentage gainers and losers, and so forth. They also talk with, and often quote in their stories, Wall Street analysts and investment advisers who serve both as news sources and commentators. Naturally, it makes sense to read the section of the market story devoted to individual stocks and industry groups for explanations of why any securities in which you are interested might have risen or fallen in price.

These roundup stories have their limitations, as most of the people who write them will readily acknowledge. Activity in an institution as large, diverse, and complex as the securities markets is not easily summarized in a few hundred, or even a few thousand words. Many analysts who provide background information and quoted commentary for these stories have their own special biases about what makes the market tick. When they comment on the future of the market, they almost always seem to see great things ahead. Their employers do not pay them to spread gloom.

As hard as Wall Street writers might strive for perspective, these stories also tend to have a short-term orientation, while most individuals are operating from a longer-term viewpoint. Yesterday, it often seems, stock prices rose because falling interest rates raised hopes of a future improvement in economic activity. The day before, stocks dropped because falling interest rates raised fears that weak demand for credit signaled a worsening economy.

One day, the story might say that a negative news development caused the market to fall. The next day, the story might say that the market "shrugged off" a similar bit of bad news. The late Sam Shulsky, a noted financial columnist who covered the stock market at one stage of his career, once confessed, "I found myself using the word 'despite' all the time."

So the 15-Minute Investor does not take the daily or weekly story on the doings of the markets as the last and complete word on what is taking place on Wall Street. Nevertheless, in addition to recounting the highlights of a day's activity in the market, the article can provide a starting point for your own thinking about investment trends.

Give a moment's consideration to the seemingly contradictory situation cited a couple of paragraphs back. If investors are selling on negative news, it would seem that as a group they are taking it seriously, and are in a generally pessimistic mood. If the market is "shrugging off" bad news, perhaps it is a sign that the bad news is already reflected in stock prices, and that investors are beginning to look for reasons (or excuses, if you like) to buy rather than to sell.

Though you may have neither the means nor the inclination to be a trader in bonds, currencies, or commodities, stories on these markets can also be sources of helpful information. The bond and money markets are constantly engaged in the process of setting levels of interest rates, which can exert a powerful influence on the stock market and your own investment plans. By following the bond market, you can seek some guidelines in making decisions about not only stocks, but other interest-bearing investments—for instance, whether to keep a cash reserve in a short-term money market fund or account, or to move it into a longer-term bank certificate of deposit or Treasury security.

The ups and downs of the dollar against foreign currencies can also influence the course of interest rates and stocks. If you own stock of a company that does a large amount of international business, you may want to be sensitive to the substantial impact foreign-exchange trends may have on the company and its profitability.

Changing commodity prices can be very important for companies that either produce, or consume as raw materials, items such as copper, cocoa, or wheat. Many professionals in the stocks and bonds business watch commodity prices closely for early clues to possible changes in the rate of inflation. Among all the commodities traded around the world, gold commands the most attention from people who are not active commodity traders. Beyond its status as an industrial commodity, gold has served for years as a kind of reverse measure of confidence in governments, paper currencies, and the stability of the international financial system. Traditionally, when the price of gold moves up strongly, fear and uncertainty are on the rise. A stagnant or declining gold market implies a measure of confidence that world events and economies are proceeding, if not perfectly, at least tolerably well.

CHAPTER THREE

INDIVIDUAL INVESTMENTS

STOCKS

Armed with a general view of what has taken place in the world and the markets, the 15-Minute Investor moves on to the alphabetical tables for stocks listed on the New York and American stock exchanges and the over-the-counter market to check on individual securities owned or being monitored. Depending on their space limitations and other requirements and preferences, individual newspapers publish tables containing varying degrees of information. But the following line is typical:

52-Week High	Low	Stock	Div	Yld %	PE Ratio	Sales 100s	High	Low	Close	Net Chg
32¼	24	Hypthcl	1.00	3.3	12	1125	30⅞	29⅝	30½	+½

Hypothetical Industries, traded on the New York Stock Exchange, is the first one you consult, since you own a fair amount of it already and are considering buying more.

> 32¼ 24 Hypthcl 1.00 3.3 12 1125 30⅞ 29⅝ **30½** **+½**

Once you spot Hypthcl in the column, you read first the numbers on the far right: 30½, its closing price of $30.50 a share, and + ½, which represents a 50-cent net gain from the previous day's close. It is only human nature to check the price before getting into the other details. Then you scan back to the beginning of the line.

32¼ 24 Hypthcl **1.00** 3.3 12 1125 30⅞ 29⅝ 30½ + ½

The first two numbers tell you that Hypothetical's highest price in the past fifty-two weeks was $32.25 a share, and its lowest $24. The annual dividend rate is $1 a share, based on the company's payment of 25-cents-a-share dividends in each of the past four quarters. If the dividend had been irregular from quarter to quarter, totaling $1, the footnote "E" would appear next to the number, denoting "Declared or paid in the past twelve months." If there were some other special circumstances affecting the dividend, such as an extra payout declared at some recent time, the number would be accompanied by another letter directing your attention to a footnote accompanying the tables. These footnotes will be discussed in more detail later in this section.

32¼ 24 Hypthcl 1.00 **3.3** 12 1125 30⅞ 29⅝ 30½ + ½

The next number, 3.3, shows the percentage annual yield the dividend provides based on the closing price of the stock. Hypothetical's yield is relatively low—a negative point to consider for investors interested in high current income, but no particular problem for people interested in it primarily as a source of potential gain from an increase in the stock's price. If there is no dividend paid, there is of course no yield, and both spaces would be blank in the table.

The absence of a dividend may indicate that the company in question is in sufficient trouble that it cannot pay one. Or it may merely be a sign that the company is relatively new and small, and is aiming for rapid growth by plowing all its earnings back into expansion plans. No matter what the reason, a stock paying no dividend is a poor candidate for the portfolios of investors whose primary objective is to earn a current return on their money to meet their living expenses.

32¼ 24 Hypthcl 1.00 3.3 **12** 1125 30⅞ 29⅝ 30½ +½

To the right of the yield figure is the price-earnings ratio. Mathematically, this number is Hypothetical's current stock price divided by the company's earnings per share reported over the past four quarters (one year, but not necessarily a calendar year). The PE, as it is known in Wall Street shorthand, is a common standard for measuring the amount of investor enthusiasm that is already reflected in the stock's price.

If the PE is high by comparison to most other stocks, it indicates that investors expect the company's earnings to grow rapidly in the future. Therefore, they are willing to "buy" the company's current capacity to make money for a high price. Conversely, a low PE tells you that the stock is out of favor for one reason or another. Earnings and other financial data can tell you a lot about the quality of a company as an investment. But a measure like the price-earnings ratio can be used to tell you whether that quality is for sale at a price that represents a good value for your money.

What constitutes a "high" or "low" PE? There is no absolute answer to that question. In the early 1960s, 20 to 1 was not unusual. A little more than a decade later, after a severe bear market, 7 to 1 or 8 to 1 was a common level. By the mid-1980s, the average ratio was back up to about 12 to 1, or precisely where Hypothetical's stands.

As basic as it may be, many Wall Street veterans say the price-earnings ratio of a given stock, or group of stocks, is only one of many things an investor should consider in making decisions. However, others have made a specialty of studying stocks with low PEs, looking for situations in which they feel a company's prospects have been overlooked by the market.

32¼ 24 Hypthcl 1.00 3.3 12 **1125** 30⅞ 29⅝ 30½ + ½

After checking the PE, the investor's eye moves on to 1125, the volume of shares traded in hundreds (in other words, 112,500 shares). If the volume figure is especially large, or differs markedly from recent levels, the investor may regard it as potentially significant. Unusual volume suggests that something is afoot. Perhaps some large investing institutions are buying or dumping the stock. Or there could be rumors of some important impending development at the company.

The various stock exchanges and other regulatory organizations in the securities industry have rules prohibiting their members from spreading rumors for their own gain. Trading on "inside information" that has not been disclosed to the public is against the law, and the Securities and Exchange Commission has run a much-publicized enforcement campaign in recent years against this kind of abuse.

But the fact remains that activity in a stock frequently increases before some significant news announcement is made. In their surveillance departments, the exchanges use computers to monitor changing volume trends closely. Alert individual investors also keep a close eye on volume, as well as price changes, in stocks they own or have an interest in.

Next to the volume figure may appear the letter "U" or "D." U signifies that the stock traded during the day or week covered by the table at a new high for at least the last fifty-two weeks. D denotes a new fifty-two-week low.

32¼ 24 Hypthcl 1.00 3.3 12 1125 **30⅞ 29⅝ 30½** + ½

The remaining figures show the highest, lowest, and last prices at which the stock traded during the period covered by the table. In the course of that trading period, Hypothetical changed hands for as much as $30.87 a share, and as little as $29.62, before closing at $30.50, up 50 cents from its previous close. The range over which a stock trades on any given day depends on several factors. If the market as a whole experiences wide swings, it will naturally tend to increase the distance between the high and low for a stock like Hypothetical.

The range might also be wide in cases where news affecting Hypothetical's business breaks in the middle of a session. In today's world of instant communications, traders might quickly respond to news they interpret as negative by dumping a stock. Within a couple of hours, Wall Street analysts might issue statements asserting that the market has exaggerated the importance of, or otherwise misinterpreted, the news in question, thus prompting buyers to step in and bid the stock up again.

Investors look at the high and low figures most closely on days when they themselves have bought or sold Hypothetical shares. They do so as a check on their broker's skill and diligence in "execution"—obtaining the best price possible for their customers.

Now to throw you a bit of a curve. As this book was being written, The Associated Press, which supplies stock tables to most of the nation's (and the world's) newspapers from a computer center in New York, was preparing to offer the tables to newspapers in a more flexible format, permitting them to publish the data in a way such as this:

Stock	Last Wk's Close	Net Chg.	Last Wk's High	Low	Sales 100s	52-wk High	Low	Div.	Yld.	PE Ratio
Hypthcl	$30^1/_2$	$+^1/_2$	$30^7/_8$	$29^5/_8$	1125	$32^1/_4$	24	1.00	3.3	12

On a few moments' inspection, you can see that the information is the same. It has simply been arranged in a different, perhaps more logical order, putting the data of most immediate interest—the stock price and net change—next to the company's name rather than at the far right.

The Hypothetical line in the above discussion is relatively simple. But as a quick glance at any actual stock table will tell you, the lists aren't generally so clear and clean. They're liberally sprinkled with shorthand symbols like pfA, wi, wt, x or x-div, vj, s and so forth. In most cases, these signify stocks that are traded under other than usual circumstances, or types of securities other than common stocks. Many of them refer you to a set of footnotes tucked in somewhere at the bottom of the stocklist pages.

You can, of course, refer to that list as individual situations arise that warrant it. But finding it and searching out the appropriate footnote is an unproductive use of a big chunk of the 15 minutes you have to work with. Better, perhaps, to become familiar enough with at least the most commonly used abbreviations and footnotes so that you don't have to look them up each time you encounter them.

Hypthcl pf is a preferred stock issued by Hypothetical—a security that carries a fixed dividend commitment which normally must be satisfied by Hypothetical's Board of Directors each quarter before they can declare a dividend on the common stock (hence the name "preferred"). **Hypthcl pfA** would indicate one of a series of preferred stocks that Hypothetical has outstanding, designated by letter sequence. **Hypthcl 4.4pf** or **Hypthcl pf4.40** shows the specific dividend rate, and may be used to distinguish it from other Hypothetical preferreds traded in the same marketplace.

Preferreds are almost always less actively traded than the common stocks of their issuers. In recent years, because of a wrinkle in the tax laws, corporate investors have been much more likely than individuals to buy and own preferred stocks.

Hypthcl wt is not a stock, but a warrant—a security issued by the company giving you the right to buy its stock for a specified price within a stated period of time. Warrants pay no dividends. **Hypthcl un** would be a package of securities, such as common stock and warrants, trading as a unit.

Hypthcl wi (when issued) or **Hypthcl wd** (when distributed) would signify a security that has not yet been issued or distributed, but has already begun trading in the market. For example, assume that Hypothetical is planning to split its stock two-for-one, that is, to distribute an additional share for each one now outstanding. Trading in the new shares sometimes begins before they are actually issued. Under usual circumstances, the new stock would logically trade at about half the price of the old. So in the table you might see Hypthcl with a last price of 30½, and just below it Hypthcl wi with a last price of about 15¼.

After the split, the stock would revert to a single listing, **Hypthcl s,** to signify that a split or stock dividend of at least 25 percent (equivalent to a five-for-four split) has occurred in the past fifty-two weeks. The fifty-two-week high and low prices for such a stock are adjusted for the effects of the stock dividend or split. If Hypothetical had begun trading for the first time in its present market less than fifty-two weeks ago, it would appear as **Hypthcl n.**

Let's say, now, that one day in the course of your 15-minute rounds of the newspaper you look up the company and find it listed as **vjHypthcl.** The "vj" conveys the unhappy news that the company in question is bankrupt, is in receivership, or has made some other filing under the Federal bankruptcy laws seeking protection from its creditors.

Why "vj"? The standard Wall Street symbol designating bankruptcy proceedings is "q," a letter which is still used by some financial reporting services. At the Associated Press, however, the letter q once caused a lot of trouble. In the pre-computer days now fading fast into history, when stock tables were produced manually, a luckless teletype operator inadvertently punched a q next to the name of a large enterprise that was most definitely not in bankruptcy proceedings. This big little error found its way into print, to the dismay of all parties concerned. To prevent a recurrence, a symbol was sought that would be difficult to type by mistake. The choice was vj.

On occasion, the "sales" item in Hypothetical's line in the table might show up, not as 1125, but as **x1125.** The "x" means "ex-dividend," or "without the dividend." In other words, as of trading on the day or week covered by the table, investors who buy the stock are ineligible to receive a specified dividend that had been declared previously by the company.

Hypothetical presently pays dividends at the rate of $1 per share annually. So a quarterly payout would be 25 cents a share. When the stock begins trading on the ex-dividend date, the market theoretically adjusts its price downward to compensate for the loss of the dividend—in this case by a quarter of a point. This adjustment is taken into account in calculating the stock's net change for the day. Thus, if Hypothetical rose to 30½ on the ex-dividend date from 30 the previous day, and the dividend was 25 cents a share, the net change would not be + ½, but rather + ¾.

Most of the other standard footnotes in the stock tables cover special circumstances involving the dividend. For example, the letter "a" tells you that the company has a regular rate, but also declares extra payouts from time to time. An "e" indicates that the amount listed was declared or paid in the past twelve months, but is not necessarily a standard rate that applies in the future. A "c" means that the payout is a liquidating dividend—such as a partial disbursement of cash proceeds realized as a company goes about the process of dismantling itself. There are numerous others for special circumstances—for instance, a "g" marks a security whose earnings are reported and dividends declared in Canadian money, but which trades in U.S. dollars. Because of the currency difference, no price-earnings ratio or yield figure is shown.

All of the foregoing discussion applies to stocks traded on the New York Stock Exchange (NYSE), the American Stock Exchange, and regional exchanges around the country. It also applies to many stocks traded in the over-the-counter market, which qualify for the National Association of Securities Dealers' National Market System. However, information on smaller over-the-counter stocks is reported in a somewhat different way.

Trading at a stock exchange takes place through a specialist, a designated broker who acts as a meeting point for all buy and sell orders on the exchange floor. In the over-the-counter market, by contrast, that business is handled by competing dealers in various locations who are linked electronically through a system called National Association of Securities Dealers Automated Quotations, or NASDAQ for short.

Rather than prices of actual transactions, the NASDAQ list for smaller over-the-counter stocks reports the highest price (bid) for which a dealer in the system was willing to buy the stock in question, and the lowest price (asked) for which a dealer was willing to sell the stock. If Hypothetical's stock traded under those circumstances, its line would look something like this:

		Sales 100s	Bid	Asked	Chg.
Hypthcl	1.00	1125	30⅛	31⅛	+½

The stock's name is followed by the annual dividend and the trading volume (sales) figure in hundreds of shares. The remaining numbers are the latest "bid" and "asked" figures, followed by the net change in the bid from the previous day (or week if it is a weekly table). Though the last actual trade might have taken place at 30½, that information is not reported. The less actively traded an over-the-counter stock is, the wider the spread between the bid and asked prices is likely to be.

The spread is how dealers get paid for making markets in over-the-counter stocks and taking the risks involved. Competition among dealers is designed to keep spreads relatively narrow. Exchange specialists, operating under the rules that cover their activities, also maintain spreads. The exchanges and the NASD each contend that their way of doing things is the better, fairer system. But whether it is a specialist broker or an over-the-counter dealer that handles your order to buy or sell, that broker or dealer is in business to make money.

There are so many stocks traded over-the-counter that it is impracticable for newspapers to report on them all. For price and other information on the smallest, least actively traded issues, you must consult a broker or otherwise obtain access to the so-called "pink sheets" distributed among investment firms that contain the latest available data on these securities.

MUTUAL FUNDS

Along with, or instead of, individual stocks, millions of investors own mutual funds. These funds are companies that pool money from their shareholders and invest it in stocks, bonds, or other securities, thus permitting individuals to put relatively small amounts of money in a diversified portfolio of investments.

Unlike stocks, the value of a mutual fund's shares is not set by open bidding among buyers and sellers. Rather, it is determined by adding up the aggregate value of the fund's portfolio at any given time, and dividing the resulting total by the number of fund shares outstanding. This is known as the net asset value (NAV) per share.

A section of the newspaper tables reporting on mutual funds might look like this:

	NAV	Buy	Chg.
Imaginary Funds Group			
Bonanza	12.20	13.02	−.12
GrInc	13.23	14.46	−.03
Income	11.97	13.08	−.04
MunBd	10.25	10.68	−.02
SpclSit	7.88	8.61	+.01
US Gov	8.80	9.41	−.04
Impetuous Fd	18.41	NL	+.11

Imaginary is a typical "family of funds," offering investors a selection of several separate funds investing in various types of securities with varying objectives. Imaginary's Bonanza Fund invests in small, speculative stocks in the hope of realizing large capital gains. Its latest net asset value is $12.20 a share. That is the price you would have received if you redeemed, or cashed in, shares of the fund on the day covered by the table. If you instead bought new shares of the fund, the price would have been

$13.02. The last figure on the line is the net change in the net asset value since the previous day's close.

The difference between the net asset value and the offering price is a sales charge. Imaginary operates "load" funds, which charge investors up-front commissions of up to 8.5 percent when they buy. The Impetuous Fund, run by a different sponsor, is "no-load" (as indicated by the symbol NL in the offering price column). It both sells and redeems shares at the net asset value, charging no commission when you buy.

On the day covered by the table, the Bonanza fund's volatile portfolio declined more than that of many other funds (it would, one hopes, go up faster than others on a better day for stock prices). The Imaginary Growth and Income Fund (GrInc), with a more staid portfolio, showed a smaller loss. The net asset values of the Imaginary Income Fund, invested entirely in bonds and high-yielding stocks; the Imaginary Municipal Bond Fund (MunBd); and the Imaginary Government Securities Fund (US Gov) all declined as well. In the modern world of volatile interest rates, even "conservative" investments like these can experience substantial price fluctuations.

Imaginary's Special Situations Fund (SpclSit), which looks for opportunities in out-of-the-way places in the stock market, managed to post a gain on a day when most other securities declined. Because of its different-drummer approach, it also might show losses on days when "the market" is up. It was a similar story with the Impetuous Fund.

One further point about no-load funds. The once-simple distinction between load and no-load funds has been blurred in recent years with the development of new fees that some funds may impose. Now there are "low load" funds, and no-load funds that may collect such exotic charges as redemption fees, contingent deferred sales commissions, or 12b-1 assessments.

As in many other types of investments, costs are generally described as a secondary consideration when you choose a mutual fund. Performance is the main concern. If a fund with minimal costs and expenses earns a 10 percent return, while a high-cost fund brings in 20 percent, you logically are happy to be with the 20-percent performer, paying the extra charges without much complaint.

But since past performance is no guarantee of future results, there is no way an investor can know for certain beforehand what an investment in any given fund will return after you buy its shares. So in a situation where you find two or more funds that seem to have approximately equal performance prospects, it makes sense to choose the one with the lowest costs.

So-called low loads set sales charges of 1, 2, or 3 percent to cover their marketing expenses. Redemption fees, by contrast, are collected at the back end—when you cash in your investment. Contingent deferred sales commissions are also charged when you redeem shares. They typically are set on a scale that diminishes the longer you keep your money in a fund, and disappear after a specified period of several years. Funds may set these charges as a way to compensate their sales forces, and at the same time to discourage frequent in-and-out trading by their shareholders.

As for 12b-1, it is the technical name for plans, authorized by the Securities and Exchange Commission in 1980, in which managements can take money from the assets of a fund to pay for marketing and distribution. "In other words," pointed out the United Mutual Fund Selector, an investment advisory service, "instead of paying a load up front, shareholders of such funds are paying an annual and ongoing charge. Unfortunately, it is often difficult for investors to determine whether or not a fund utilizes a 12b-1 plan. Many times this information is buried in the back of the prospectus or is in the 'statement of additional information.' ''

BONDS

When they invest in bonds, most individual investors do so for the long term, intending to hold them to maturity. But particularly in the last decade, during which interest rates have fluctuated widely, prices of bonds have moved up and down regularly, just like stocks. Many large newspapers carry daily and weekly tables covering trading of bonds listed on stock exchanges, U.S. government securities traded over-the-counter, and perhaps some other interest-bearing securities such as federal agency bonds. A knowledge of how to read the bond tables can help the 15-Minute Investor not only to monitor prices of individual bonds, but also to keep tabs on trends in interest rates.

There are many types of bonds and other interest-bearing securities. Unfortunately for the newcomer, the markets for the various classes of them tend to differ in the way they operate. As a result, the table for government bonds is arranged differently from the table for corporate bonds. Within the government securities group, Treasury bond tables differ from those for Treasury bills. This means that inexperienced readers must spend some time acquainting themselves with the various tables before they can consult them as quickly and easily as they check the stock tables.

An outstanding bond of Hypothetical Corp. would look, in the listed bond tables, much like a stock quotation:

Bond	Current Yield	Sales in $1000s	High	Low	Last	Net Chg
Hypthcl 12s03	13.5	21	88⅞	88⅝	88⅞	+½

This is a bond issued some time in the past by Hypothetical, with a stated interest rate of 12 percent, due to mature in the year 2003.

Hypthcl 12s03   13.5   21   **88⅞   88⅝   88⅞   +½**

Its price is quoted in dollars per $100 in face value. The highest price for the day covered by the table was $88.87, the lowest $88.62, and the last $88.87, up 50 cents from the previous day. The bond is trading at a discount from "par," or 100, for any of several reasons—because prevailing interest rates have risen since the date the bond was issued, because investors believe the risk that Hypothetical might default has increased since the issue date, or a combination of those two factors.

In any case, if you were to buy Hypothetical bonds now, you could get $100 face amount for about $88.87. So the effective yield you would receive on the nominal 12 percent interest paid on the bond would be higher.

Hypthcl 12s03 **13.5 21** 88⅞ 88⅝ 88⅞ + ½

It would be 13.5 percent, listed in the first column next to the description of the bond under the heading "current yield." The adjoining figure, 21, is the amount of bonds traded, in thousands of dollars—that is, $21,000 in face amount of the bonds were traded on the day covered by the table.

If there were no current yield shown, but the symbol "cv" appeared in its place, you would know that the bond was convertible into stock, in most cases the common stock of the issuer, in this case Hypothetical Corp. A convertible is a hybrid form of security that behaves in some ways like a bond, and in some ways like a stock. Many individual investors have an active interest in convertibles.

If Hypothetical were in any form of bankruptcy proceedings, its bonds, like its stock, would carry the notation "vj" before the company's name.

Trading in bonds and other interest-bearing securities issued by the Federal government takes place in a separate, specialized over-the-counter market. Information on trading in these securities is reported, naturally enough, in a separate, special table under the heading "Government Securities" or "Treasury Bills, Bonds and Notes." A small slice of that table might look something like this:

Date	Rate	Bid	Asked	Chg.	Yield
Aug 03	11⅛	105.22	105.30	+.10	10.39
Nov 03	11⅞	111.18	111.26	+.7	10.42

When you move from the stock and corporate bond markets—where the usual minimum price fluctuation is one-eighth of a point—to the government bond market, you must mentally shift gears to think in thirty-seconds of a point, rather than eighths.

The U.S. Treasury bond maturing in August 2003 carries a nominal interest rate of 11⅛ percent. Since the time of its issue, interest rates have fallen, and the bond is trading at a premium to par, or 100. The latest dealer bid price for the August 03s was 105²²⁄₃₂, or about $105.69, for every $100 in face value. The latest dealer asked price was 105³⁹⁄₃₂. On the day in question, the bid price increased ¹⁰⁄₃₂ from the previous day. The bond below it in the table, maturing in November 2003, rose ⁷⁄₃₂ over the same span. At their current asked price, the August 03s offer an effective annual yield of 10.39 percent, while the November 03s return 10.42 percent. Government bonds with lives from their issue date of two to ten years are called notes and are flagged with the letter "n" next to the maturity date.

Government securities with lives as short as three months to a year are called Treasury bills. These securities provide for no periodic interest payments, but are issued at a discount from their face value and redeemed on maturity at their face value, with the difference constituting the interest received by their owners. Because they work this way, they are quoted not in dollar prices, but in terms of their interest rates, like this:

Date	Bid	Asked	Chg.	Yield
Dec 12	6.92	6.90	+0.07	7.24
Dec 26	6.85	6.81	.....	7.15

The Treasury bill table shows bid and asked interest rates for bills maturing on Dec. 12 and Dec. 26 of the current year, followed by the daily net change on the interest rate and the effective annual yield. If you want to convert the bid and asked figures into "prices," you can simply subtract from 100. Thus a dealer was, in effect, willing to pay $93.08 (100 minus 6.92) for every $100 in face value to buy Dec. 12 bills, or to sell the same bills for $93.10 (100 minus 6.90)

If some of these technical points are beyond your interest or concern, you can simply look at the last column of figures—the yield. For practical purposes, this shows the prevailing level of returns available on Treasury bills, which serve as a sort of standard for many other short-term interest rates.

Why is the yield different from the stated interest rate on $100? Because the buyer of $100 in face amount of Treasury bills puts up less than $100. To consider a relatively simple example, suppose you bought a $10,000 bill for $9,000, waited exactly a year until it matured, and received a payment of $10,000 in cash. That's $1,000 interest on an investment of $9,000, for an annual yield of 11.11 percent (not 10 percent).

MONEY MARKET FUNDS AND ACCOUNTS

Many newspapers carry weekly tables on money market mutual funds and bank money-market deposit accounts that are of special interest to individual investors. These funds and accounts are a popular place for people to put the portion of their assets that they wish to maintain as a cash reserve.

Fund	Assets ($million)	Avg. Mat.	7-Day Yld.	30-Day Yld.
Example MMTrst	620	37	7.20	7.40
Example GvTrst	1552	32	6.95	7.02
Extra Cash Rsv	89	49	7.31	7.41

In this illustration of a money fund table, the Example Money Market Trust has assets of $620 million (620, in millions). The securities in its portfolio—such as large bank certificates of deposit, commercial paper issued by corporations, and other short-term interest-bearing investments—have an average of thirty-seven days left before they reach maturity. The fund's yield, calculated at an annual rate, for the past seven days was 7.20 percent. Over the past thirty days, the annualized yield was 7.40 percent.

The Example Government Securities Trust seeks an added

measure of safety by investing its assets only in short-term securities of the Federal government and its agencies. This type of money fund is highly popular (note that assets of Example's government fund are more than twice as large as those of its sister fund). Note also that investors pay a price for its presumed greater safety, in the form of a lower yield—6.95 percent over the past seven days, 7.02 percent over the past thirty.

Of the three funds in the table, the Extra Cash Reserve Fund has the highest yields for both periods. One reason for that may be that it has the longest average portfolio maturity—forty-nine days. As a comparison of the seven-day and thirty-day yields of all three funds indicates, interest rates have been declining in the period covered by the table.

Money fund yields tend to lag behind movements of interest rates in the credit markets because the funds' returns are determined by securities they bought a few days or a few weeks earlier. The longer the maturity of a given fund's portfolio, the greater the lag time. Thus, in periods of falling rates, funds with relatively long maturities tend to be the most rewarding investments. Conversely, when rates are rising, funds with the shortest maturities are likely to be the first to respond.

A separate section of the money fund table provides listings for tax-free funds—those that invest in short-term securities of state and local governments, the interest on which is exempt from federal income taxes. Unlike other mutual fund tables, the money fund tables do not carry figures for net asset value per share, since these funds normally keep their NAVs constant at a figure of, say, $1 per share.

Also carried weekly in some newspapers is a report from the Bank Rate Monitor of North Palm Beach, Florida, of representative yields available on bank money-market deposit accounts and six-month certificates of deposit. This provides a useful comparison in your shopping for the best return on your money. However, no data for money market investments should be taken as any assurance of future results, since money market conditions and yields are constantly changing.

CHAPTER FOUR

MARKET
STATISTICS

Once the 15-Minute Investor has checked the top news of the day, the market roundups and individual securities of interest, the next step is a review of the latest statistics and other measures of overall activity in the stock market. Some of these are familiar to just about everyone; others are relatively obscure, and their potential uses may not be widely understood. The point of this exercise is to determine not only what the market as a whole is doing, but what subtle trends are taking place beneath the surface.

The effort to summarize in numerical form what is taking place in the market dates back a long time. The first Dow Jones stock averages appeared in the late 1800s. Almost a century later, Dow Jones's average of 30 industrials remains the best known measure of market activity. But today there are many others whose sponsors claim they offer not only a broader, but also a more accurate and meaningful measurement of the state of the market than "the Dow" can provide.

No matter how a market average or index is computed, it cannot tell you much about which individual stocks and stock groups are performing best and getting the most attention at any given time. Thus, the 15-Minute Investor's survey of market indicators should also include the lists of the most active stocks in the various markets, of the stocks which had the biggest percentage gains and losses, and of issues reaching new highs and lows for the past fifty-two weeks.

THE DOW JONES AVERAGES:

Dow Jones & Co., publisher of the *Wall Street Journal,* compiles a series of four stock market averages: (1) 30 industrial stocks, (2) 20 transportation issues, (3) 15 utilities, and (4) a composite of all 65 of those stocks. The four averages are published daily in most newspapers, and may be calculated at any time by anyone who knows the most recent prices of the component stocks.

The industrial average, for all the criticism it receives, is still the standard most commonly used by the press, the public, and a great many Wall Streeters in discussing stocks. When the question is asked "What did the market do today?," and the reply comes, "Up a little more than six," the answerer is implicitly understood to be referring to the Dow. When brokers and investment advisers have a market forecast that they wish to communicate with maximum public impact, they usually speak in terms of the Dow.

The transportation average, though not as well known, is also widely watched on Wall Street. It began life as the rail average, but was modified in the 1960s to include airlines and trucking companies as well as railroad operators. Today it represents "the wings and wheels of the market," in the words of Newton Zinder, a widely respected market analyst. After all, transportation industries represent the circulatory system of the American economy, carrying freight of all descriptions, business travelers, and people on vacations and other personal trips. Followers of a venerable school of thought known as the Dow theory watch the transportation average to see if it "confirms" what the industrial average is doing by joining the industrials at a new high or low.

The utility average, once largely neglected, comes under close scrutiny these days as well. Stocks of electric and natural gas utilities are highly sensitive to changing interest-rate expectations, because companies in those industries tend to be heavy borrowers of capital, and because utility stocks traditionally are owned by yield-conscious investors. Many Wall Streeters refer to utility stocks as "bond substitutes." To the extent that they anticipate forthcoming changes in interest rates, utility stocks can serve as a rough advance indicator of where the stock market as a whole might be heading. In 1985, when the Dow Jones utility average surpassed a record high set more than two decades earlier, it created a good deal of excitement among followers of the stock market.

The 65-stock composite average, though regularly reported along with the others, does not have much of a following on Wall Street or with the investing public. It's a good bet that even an ardent follower of the stock market will be unable to tell you where that particular average stands without looking it up.

Although you may sometimes hear Dow Jones's figures described as indexes, that term is incorrect. An index is based on an arbitrary reference point. The Dow Jones numbers, by contrast, are averages of the actual prices of their component stocks. In its simplest form, an average of 30 stocks is calculated by adding up the prices of those individual issues, and then dividing by 30.

In practice, the Dow Jones divisors have had to be changed many times over the years to reflect changes in the makeup of a given average and such developments as stock splits by component companies. To see why this is necessary, consider a case in which one of the Dow 30 paid a two-for-one stock split, lowering the price of its shares from about $100 to about $50 in the process. If no change were made in the divisor, the average would show a large, artificial decline. To avert this distortion, the divisor must be reduced by an amount equal to the effect of the split. As of mid-1985, the divisors were 1.116 for the industrial average, 1.068 for the transportation average, 2.437 for the utility average, and 4.718 for the 65-stock composite.

It was mentioned above that the Dow Jones averages, and particularly the 30 industrials, have long been the subject of much criticism and debate. What's all the fuss about? For one thing, students of the market complain, no sample of just 30 stocks can give a consistently accurate picture of what's happening to the thousands of issues that trade every business day.

It is often remarked that the Dow Jones industrial average can be misleading because it is made up mostly of older, long-established companies that have passed their years of fastest growth. For many years now, the greatest growth in the U.S. economy has been in the service, rather than the industrial sector. Defenders of the Dow counter by pointing out that the average has been modernized in recent years by the addition of companies like Merck, in pharmaceuticals, and American Express, the big financial services concern. They also say that officials of Dow Jones have been rightly cautious in minimizing the number of changes in the average's makeup, in order to emphasize continuity and avoid chasing after fads or other short-term changes in business and financial trends.

Some people don't like the fact that the industrial average, with its simple makeup, gives more weight to changes in its higher-priced component stocks than their lower-priced counterparts. Suppose you owned 100 shares of a stock traded at $100, and 400 shares of a stock traded at $25. If the $100 stock drops to $96 and the $25 stock rises to $26, the overall effect on your net worth is zero. You had equal amounts of money invested in securities that rose and fell, respectively, by 4 percent. But if the two stocks were in the Dow Jones industrial average, their price changes would lower the average by 2.69 points, since one took a drop of $4 while the other rose only $1.

Another objection raised by many observers is that the Dow Jones averages do not take a company's total market value into account. If there are 100 million shares outstanding of one $50 stock, and 50 million of another issue also trading at $50, the first represents twice as much wealth as the second. But in the Dow Jones averages, the two would carry equal weight.

On many occasions in the past, a big swing in the price of a single component stock has resulted in a daily reading for the Dow Jones industrial average that exaggerated the market's strength or weakness. Alert commentators have pointed this out in the course of their discussion of the market's doings. All these questions, however, haven't done much to change the Dow's status as a popular symbol of "the market."

Component stocks for the Dow Jones averages as of late 1985:

Industrials

Allied-Signal
Aluminum Co. of America
American Can
American Express
American Telephone & Telegraph
Bethlehem Steel
Chevron
DuPont
Eastman Kodak
Exxon
General Electric
General Motors
Goodyear
Inco
International Business Machines
International Harvester
International Paper
McDonald's
Merck & Co.
Minnesota Mining & Manufacturing
Owens-Illinois
Philip Morris
Procter & Gamble

Sears Roebuck
Texaco
Union Carbide
United Technologies
United States Steel
Westinghouse Electric
F. W. Woolworth

Transportation

AMR Corp.
American President
Burlington Northern
Canadian Pacific
Carolina Freight
Consolidated Freightways
CSX Corp.
Delta Air Lines
Eastern Airlines
Federal Express
Norfolk Southern
NWA Inc.
Overnite Transportation
Pan Am Corp.
Santa Fe Southern Pacific
Transway International
Trans World Airlines
UAL Inc.
Union Pacific
USAir Group

Utilities

American Electric Power
Cleveland Electric Illuminating
Columbia Gas System
Commonwealth Edison
Consolidated Edison of New York

Consolidated Natural Gas
Detroit Edison
Houston Industries
Niagara Mohawk Power
Pacific Gas & Electric
Panhandle Eastern
Peoples Energy
Philadelphia Electric
Public Service Electric & Gas
Southern California Edison

STANDARD & POOR'S STOCK INDEXES

Standard & Poor's Corp., the large financial rating and advisory firm, calculates and reports each business day an index of 500 stocks. It also breaks down this composite into several component groups: 400 industrials, 40 utilities, 20 transportation stocks, and 40 financial issues.

The S&P 500 is not as well known to the public as its older rival, the Dow Jones industrial average. However, it is widely used by professional investors as the yardstick against which they measure the investment results they achieve. When the government makes its monthly report on the index of leading economic indicators (discussed in the section of this book on Economic Statistics), it uses the S&P 500 as one of the twelve components of the index.

Standard & Poor's produced its first index of stock price movements in 1917. The 500-stock composite index was developed in 1957. Like other indexes (as opposed to averages such as the Dow Jones industrials), it uses a chosen base period in the past as an arbitrary reference point. The 500's base is set at average prices in 1941–43, equal to an index reading of 10.

Also unlike the Dow, the 500 is "weighted"—that is, the proportionate role of each stock in the index is adjusted to conform to the number of shares outstanding. "This method of market weighting and the broad base of the S&P 500 make it a reliable measure of the aggregate movement in stock values," Standard & Poor's maintains. This weighting tends to put a heavy emphasis on the large stocks traded on the New York Stock Exchange. Indeed, most of the stocks that make up the 500 are listed on the NYSE, although a handful of American Stock Exchange and over-the-counter issues also are included. If your investments are primarily in older, established stocks, the 500 (or the 400 industrials) is a handy tool for figuring how well you are doing in comparison with "the market." If, on the other hand, you concentrate on smaller, "emerging growth" stocks, a better standard may be the NASDAQ composite index of over-the-counter stocks.

Events such as mergers or the rise of a new industry cause S&P occasionally to make changes in the components of its indexes. "An attempt is made to hold them to a minimum," the company says. Departures from and additions to the S&P 500 list can be a sensitive subject for managers of "index funds," pools of money that are set up to match the performance of the 500. These managers want to conduct as few buy and sell transactions as possible.

"When a stock is removed from the index, it is usually because a company was acquired by or merged into another," S&P says. "Occasionally, a stock will be removed because a company has financial problems or its particular subgroup is no longer representative of its industry.

"Stocks are added to the index for three reasons: (1) replacement of a dropped stock, adding the new one to the same industry group, if possible; (2) the result of periodic review which keeps industry groups up to date and refines coverage of the index; and (3) establishment of a new industry group to reflect what appears to be the development of a broad and more than transitory investor interest in the group."

In 1985, the S&P 500 set record highs above 200, representing a 1,750 percent increase since the 1941–43 base period. The all-time low? S&P calculated it retroactively to be 4.40 on June 1, 1932—in the depths of the Great Depression.

THE NEW YORK STOCK EXCHANGE INDEXES

Since 1966, the New York Stock Exchange has compiled an index of all the common stocks traded in its market. (Warrants, preferred stocks and bonds listed on the NYSE are not included.) Its base is set at 50, equal to the value of listed common stocks on Dec. 31, 1965, adjusted for subsequent listings and delistings as well as stock splits. The number 50 was chosen because it was close to the average price of stocks trading at that time.

However, the index is not based on stock prices alone, but rather on market value—that is, the price of each stock multiplied by the number of shares outstanding. The exchange also reports subindexes for four classes of stocks: industrials, transportation, utilities, and finance. Historical figures for the composite index have been calculated weekly back to 1939. Its low of 4.64 was reached in 1942. In 1985, it surpassed 100 for the first time.

As a measure of stock price trends in a single (albeit the largest) market, the NYSE composite has both its special uses and its drawbacks. By itself, it tells you relatively little about the degree of speculative activity in smaller stocks that are generally traded at the American Stock Exchange and in the over-the-counter market. But in comparison with indexes in those other marketplaces, it can provide helpful information on the kinds of stocks that are currently in vogue.

A strong showing by the NYSE composite, in a period when indexes of other markets are lagging, may be evidence that the primary force pushing the market higher is buying by investing institutions concentrating on stocks of larger, older companies. The reverse—relative strength in the Amex and over-the-counter issues—hints at speculative enthusiasm for smaller, newer companies, and perhaps a heightened degree of participation by individual investors. This is a generalization, of course, and subject to the flaws of most generalizations. In any case, the NYSE composite index is a regular fixture in most close observers' scrutiny of the stock market.

Along with its indexes, the NYSE provides the news media daily with a figure for the net change in the price of an "average" share. It is intended for use only on a day-to-day basis rather than over any extended period of time, and is not adjusted for changes in the exchange's roster of listed stocks or for stock splits. Thus it cannot be used for charts or historical comparisons. Wall Street professionals pay little heed to this number. Many large newspapers do not publish it. Unless you own that average share (which of course you don't), you are safe in ignoring it.

THE NASDAQ INDEXES FOR THE OVER-THE-COUNTER MARKET

The National Association of Securities Dealers, the industry group that oversees trading of over-the-counter stocks, established a computerized market for those issues in 1971. At that time, it introduced the NASDAQ (National Association of Securities Dealers Automated Quotations) index of over-the-counter stocks, as well as six subindexes, with a base of 100 as of Feb. 5, 1971. By the mid-1980s, the NASDAQ system had grown to become the nation's second largest securities marketplace, and had vocal aspirations to overtake the New York Stock Exchange for the Number One ranking.

With this expansion, the system has come to include a good many well-recognized corporations that could qualify for listing, if their directors and managements so chose, on stock exchanges. Nevertheless, the NASDAQ composite is still widely used as a measure of investors' enthusiasm for relatively speculative stocks—those that have not yet had the time or the good fortune to establish a long-standing reputation in the marketplace, however bright their prospects. The composite index fell as low as about 55 in the bear market of 1974. It reached a record high of 328.91 on June 24, 1983.

The NASDAQ composite includes the common stocks of all domestic companies whose shares are traded in the NASDAQ system, except for those that are also traded on one or more stock exchanges, or those that have only a single market maker (brokerage firm or other dealer that stands ready continuously to buy and sell the stock). Foreign stocks are also excluded. Since over-the-counter trading is based on bid-and-asked quotations, the price used for each stock is the prevailing lowest bid at which a dealer is willing to buy the stock. Like the S&P 500, the NYSE composite, and most other market indexes, the NASDAQ composite is weighted according to the number of shares outstanding for each stock. The six subindexes within the NASDAQ composite are the industrial, bank, insurance, other finance, transportation, and utility indexes.

As described earlier in this book, NASDAQ has developed and expanded what it calls its National Market System—a group of over-the-counter stocks for which actual prices, rather than bid-and-asked quotations, are reported in newspapers and other financial information sources. A National Market System composite index, and an industrial index, were established with a starting point of 100 on July 10, 1984. If the National Market System flourishes as much as the NASD hopes, it is possible that these two indexes will gain increasing recognition among Wall Streeters and the investing public. As of this writing, habit and common sense dictate that most investors concentrate their attention on the original NASDAQ composite index.

THE AMERICAN
STOCK EXCHANGE
MARKET VALUE
INDEX

The index published by the American Stock Exchange is often cited in tandem with the NASDAQ composite as a measure of trends in smaller stocks. It should be noted, however, that the Amex list has a heavy representation of energy and other natural resources stocks and smaller high-technology issues. Trends involving either of these special groups, which may be independent of broader market moves, can influence the picture it presents.

The market value index was introduced in 1973, with a base of 100 as of Aug. 31 of that year, replacing a "price change index" that had previously been the primary means of measuring activity on the exchange. A decade later, the market value index was adjusted to half its former value (in a move analogous to a two-for-one split of an individual stock) to make it more suitable for trading in options based on it. Thus the starting base level became 50.

It includes not only common stocks of domestic companies, but also warrants and American depositary receipts of foreign companies traded on the exchange. Excluded are preferred stocks, rights (a sort of short-term form of warrants), and securities traded on a when-issued basis before they are available for actual delivery. Like most other indexes, it is weighted according to the number of shares outstanding for each issue, and is adjusted daily so that new listings, delistings, stock splits and similar changes in its makeup do not distort it.

Unlike many other market measures such as the Dow Jones industrial average, the Amex market value index counts cash dividends paid by component companies as though they were reinvested in shares of the stocks involved. Logically, this gives the index an upward bias in comparison to other yardsticks like the Dow. The Amex says that adding in the dividends "reflects the total return of its components." In practice, many Amex stocks are young companies that pay relatively low or no dividends.

The exchange calculates eight subindexes by industry. Along with high technology and natural resources, these include capital goods (companies that sell equipment and other production facilities to other businesses); consumer goods; service; retail; financial; and housing, construction, and land development. There are also eight geographical subindexes, grouping all Amex-listed stocks by the location of their headquarters. Some newspapers may publish these as a means of tracing the stock-market fortunes of companies based in their sections of the country. Otherwise, none of the subindexes has a wide following in the financial world.

From a base of 50, the market value index got as low as about 30 in the bear market of 1974. By July of 1983, it had climbed to just under 250.

THE VALUE LINE INDEXES

The Value Line Investment Survey, the nation's largest investment advisory service, has since 1961 calculated an index of the stocks it reports on. Recently, the total was more than 1,650 issues—making the index one of the broadest measures available of stock price trends. About 80 percent of its components are New York Stock Exchange issues, but a good many stocks from the American Stock Exchange and the over-the-counter market are also represented. Most of the stocks are classified as "industrials," but there are also some 150 utilities and a few railroad issues included. In its advisory reports, the firm publishes separate industrial, utility, and rail indexes. Most newspapers carry only the composite index.

In its method of computation, this index is unique. It is a geometric average of stock prices. As the investment firm of Drexel Burnham Lambert explains, "While most index calculation methods make use of the arithmetic mean of the components' prices or market values, [Value Line's] calculation uses the geometric mean. The arithmetic mean is often referred to as an "average"; for example, the arithmetic mean of 4, 8, and 16 is 9.33, or 4 + 8 + 16 divided by 3." The geometric mean of the same three numbers, which involves some calculus that the writer presumes is of minor interest to the 15-Minute Investor, is 8.

The makeup of the Value Line composite changes whenever the firm begins analytical coverage of a new stock or stocks, or drops one or more issue from its list. Says Drexel Burnham: "Since each component is given equal weight in the index, [the Value Line composite's] performance is not dominated by the large-capitalization issues. As a result, [it] 'reads' the market differently from other broad-based indices, such as the NYSE composite or the S&P 500. It is more sensitive to the performance of smaller, 'second-tier' stocks. Therefore, [it] has not displayed a consistent correlation with the Dow Jones industrial average. In fact, there are periods when [it] and the DJIA moved in opposite directions."

THE WILSHIRE
INDEX

Wilshire Associates, an investment management firm based in Santa Monica, California, computes and reports daily an index that its sponsor says "represents the total dollar value in billions of dollars of all actively traded common stocks in the U.S." It is sometimes called the Wilshire 5,000 because of the number of stocks it originally comprised, although a data analyst at the firm reported that there were actually about 6,000 stocks in the index as of mid-1985, when it surpassed $2 trillion for the first time.

The index is often cited by people who want a measure of the total value of wealth reposing in "the stock market." It should not, however, be thought of as simply the sum of the prices of all New York Stock Exchange, American Stock Exchange, and actively traded over-the-counter stocks, multiplied by the number of shares of each stock outstanding. Rather, it is an index whose formula compensates for a changing roster of individual component stocks.

Introduced in 1974, the Wilshire Index has gained increasing recognition in the financial world in recent years. Many general interest newspapers, as well as specialized financial papers, now publish it daily. To a newcomer, the index may be a bit daunting, indicating as it does the addition or subtraction of billions of dollars each day from the aggregate portfolios of investors in this country. In comparing the Wilshire Equity Index with other market indicators, the percentage change is the key figure. As Wilshire Associates notes, "the index is more volatile than the Dow or the S&P 500 since it includes smaller, more volatile companies."

ADVANCES
AND DECLINES

Along with the stock averages and indexes, active investors make a practice of checking the figures for the markets they are interested in that show the number of issues advancing, declining, and unchanged. Compared with the mathematical complexity of some of the indexes, the advance-decline data are remarkably simple. They cannot tell you how much any given stock rose or fell, nor what types of stocks did better than others. Without some extra record-keeping on your part, they don't give you much of a basis for perspective over time. But they do provide a gauge of the general mood of investors by measuring what analysts call the market's "breadth."

Suppose, for example, that you see this table in your newspaper:

NYSE	Fri.	Thurs.
Up	976	1,211
Down	683	437
Unchanged	387	387
Issues Traded	2,046	2,035

Even without a knowledge of what any of the averages or indexes did on either of these two days, you can tell at a glance from these few raw figures that the market was strong on both. Thursday was exceptionally good, with nearly three stocks rising in price for every one that declined. Friday was a little less dramatic, but still a good showing.

Analysts generally operate on the theory that the wider the gap between advances and declines (or vice versa), the more powerful a market move is. In fact, the advance-decline figures serve as a good check on an indicator such as the Dow Jones industrial average. Let's say that the Dow gained 10 points on Thursday and another 14 on Friday. A close observer might conclude that, despite what the Dow indicated, the market actually had a better day on Thursday than it did on Friday—and, indeed, that the breadth figures for Friday might be a tipoff that the rally was starting to run out of steam.

In cases where the Dow, and perhaps the S&P 500 as well, rises sharply, but advances barely outnumber declines, market veterans tend to view the numbers with great caution. This picture suggests that buying interest is confined to a few big-name stocks, and that its lasting power is extremely suspect. It is not uncommon on relatively trendless days for the Dow and the advance-decline statistics to point in opposite directions—for example, a 2.50 rise in the Dow while declines outnumber advances 856 to 791. It is standard practice to refer to this as a ''mixed'' market.

Mixed days are sometimes just what they seem—uneventful days in which it is hard to find much of significance taking place anywhere in the market. But, odd though it may seem, many trading days in which the market finishes mixed are anything but dull. Even though they had little apparent net effect on the prices of stocks you own or are following, they may merit thorough examination for signs of such things as a change in the recent prevailing mood of investors.

The number of stocks finishing unchanged commands relatively little attention. An especially large number of unchanged issues may perhaps be spoken of by some market followers as a sign of ''investor uncertainty.'' But does that really make sense? Logically, it could be described as just the opposite—evidence that investors found the prices set in the previous trading today to be just the right balance between supply and demand, and in need of neither an increase nor a decrease.

The ''total issues traded'' is likewise of generally little interest to the 15-Minute Investor. The majority of listed common stocks on the Big Board trade just about every business day. Fluctuations in the number of total issues traded stem mainly from the degree of activity in preferred stocks and other exotica with less active markets. The issues-traded figure tends to rise near the end of the year, as investors maneuver for tax purposes. Then, and at most other points on the calendar, it does not correlate well with volume, which is a much better means of reading the intensity of activity in the market.

VOLUME

We have already talked about the significance of trading volume figures for individual securities. Of course, overall trading volume figures for the various markets are also reported daily. Brokers tend to talk about them a lot, partly because volume is very important to their business (each trade a commission brings). Beyond that, however, volume provides some vital signs of the health or ailing state of the markets. It is the subject of many theories concerning the market outlook.

Just what constitutes "heavy," "active," "moderate," "light," or "sluggish" trading? These terms are used all the time, sometimes without providing much firm information for the casual or novice follower of the markets. They are, it must be acknowledged, all relative terms that can be stretched pretty thin in hasty descriptions of market activity.

In 1975, daily volume on the New York Stock Exchange of 32 million shares was enough to set a record. A decade later, with the greatly expanded role of investing institutions in the marketplace, 90 million or 100 million was routine and would probably be widely described as "moderate." It can readily be seen that the range of "light" to "heavy" shifts with changes in the state of the markets. Thus, the terms are best defined against the background of recent trends. "Light" would be significantly below the average daily volume over the past six months or a year. "Moderate" would be close to that average. "Heavy" would portray record, or near-record, activity.

Light volume, as one might suspect, is generally regarded as a negative in all kinds of markets. Because the stock market is a secondary market for shares that have already been sold once to investors, it has a presumed continuous downward bias, however slight. To put it another way, no one is obliged to buy stock. But at any given time there is likely to be some quantity of stock that must be sold by investors who have need of their money for other purposes, whether those purposes be the purchase of a house or the settlement of estate taxes. In theory, a certain amount of volume is necessary just to absorb this supply of stock for sale if a decline in prices is to be averted.

Light volume is unimpressive in rising markets because it betokens a lack of "conviction," or true belief, among the general investing populace. Light volume is also regarded as unhealthy in declining markets, because it suggests that scarcely anybody wants to buy. When volume picks up in periods of declining prices, it may seem to be evidence that caution is evolving into fear or even panic. But heavy volume in such markets may actually be viewed as a plus by many analysts. After all, for every seller there is a buyer, and that buyer might just be the smarter of the two. In the past, markets have often been most emotional when they neared or reached extremes that became turning points.

Volume in the over-the-counter market and on the American Stock Exchange, by comparison with volume on the NYSE, provides one measure of the degree of speculative enthusiasm for newer or lower-priced stocks. Relatively heavy activity in O-T-C and Amex stocks, especially for extended periods of time, is sometimes taken as a warning of unsustainable speculative fever. Low volume in these markets for long periods suggests a cautious, conservative climate.

NEW HIGHS AND LOWS

In the market tables, you'll recall, stocks that hit new highs or lows for the past fifty-two weeks are flagged with the symbol

"U" or "D." Many newspapers also publish separate lists of the new highs and lows, and the total in each group. The total figures may appear as part of the advance-decline data, like this:

NYSE	Fri.	Thurs.
Up	976	1,211
Down	683	437
Unchanged	387	387
Issues Traded	2,046	2,035
New Highs	258	215
New Lows	8	12

Or the same numbers can be found at the head of the Highs and Lows lists, in this manner:

**NEW
HIGHS 258**
AAR
AdtLab
Adams Exp

**NEW
LOWS 8**
Acme Ind
CslC pfA

The significance of the raw total depends to a great degree on what the market has done over the past year. If it has risen over most of that period, for example, the number of new highs is very likely to exceed the number of new lows even on days of substantial market declines. Conversely, in bear markets, new lows may well predominate even after a rally has begun.

Some analysts watch the numbers most closely in times when the popular averages and indexes are making new highs or bear-market lows. If there are, say, 350, 400, or more new highs at the same time that the Dow and other indicators hit new peaks, all is presumably well. But if the number of new highs dwindles as the Dow keeps climbing, it is taken as a sign that the market's advance is starting to falter. Similarly, in down markets, a shrinking number of new lows is taken as a favorable sign.

The lists of individual stocks can yield some further helpful information at times. A quick scan of them may enable you to see a preponderance of issues from one or a few industries. For instance, if you see many familiar names from the food, soft drink, and utility industries on the New High list, you may conclude that investors are favoring conservative, or "defensive" stocks—companies whose fortunes wouldn't be drastically affected by a slowdown of the economy. If instead it is dotted with high-technology companies and perhaps some names that you don't readily recognize, it may well be that a more venturesome, ebullient mood prevails.

THE MOST-ACTIVE
LIST

A list of five to fifteen of the most actively traded stocks in each of the major markets is a staple item in the financial pages of many newspapers. It is simply a ranking of those stocks by volume of shares changing hands. Years ago, when institutions were much less a part of the stock market than they are today, many investors checked the most-active list for individual issues that were getting the most attention in the marketplace. Today, a single block trade by one institution that decides to sell or buy can catapult a stock onto the active list, without necessarily indicating that anything of more than passing significance for the stock is occurring.

Still, the most-active list may be worth inspection for the 15-Minute Investor on several counts. Writers of stock market stories for the newspaper watch it closely for individual stocks, or groups of stocks, that are moving in response to news, rumors, or perhaps a brokerage-house analyst's change of opinion.

One point some students of the market like to check is not the volume of shares traded, but rather the price changes shown by the stocks on the list. If, say, twelve of the fifteen volume leaders finish a given day with losses, it is a sign of negative sentiment that may or may not have been reflected in the other market indicators. Similarly, a preponderance of plus signs betokens strength.

Another column in the list that sometimes gets special attention is the closing prices of the most active Big Board issues. If these prices are mostly high, they suggest that the action is concentrated in blue chips and other stocks regarded as high in quality and favored by investing institutions. On the other hand, if the list includes several stocks priced under $20 a share or so, speculative activity may well be running strong. There are some big names that appear on the list with great regularity—International Business Machines, American Telephone & Telegraph, and some others. This is only natural, because they have a great many shares outstanding, and a lot of those shares are owned and traded by institutions striving to top each other in performance from quarter to quarter and year to year. So you may seek to get the greatest benefit from the most-active list by scanning it for unfamiliar or seldom-seen names.

PERCENTAGE CHANGE LEADERS

Which would you prefer—to buy 100 shares of a $50 stock that subsequently rises to $55, or to buy 100 shares of a $5 stock that subsequently rises to $10? Either way, you are $500 richer (not counting commissions and taxes). But the $50 stock produced just a 10 percent return on your investment, while the $5 stock permitted you a 100 percent return, doubling your money.

When you think along these lines, it's not the absolute dollar change, but the percentage change, that counts. A standard item in the statistical section of many newspapers is a list of ten to twenty-five top percentage gainers and losers from each of the major markets. As it is produced by computer at the Associated Press, the list is cleaned up by eliminating any stocks priced below $2, and those with trading volume of less than 1,000 shares.

On any given day, this list, like the most-active list, may contain several stocks that have felt the impact of news or rumors that warrant its inclusion in the separate stock-market story. However, it may also present several notable gainers and losers for which there is no explanation available. Quite possibly, some of these might merit further investigation on your part. A note of caution, however—by its very nature, this list emphasizes short-term swings in the prices of individual stocks. If you are investing from a longer-term perspective, you probably do not want to become overly concerned with these fluctuations. Stocks that produce outstanding returns over time often do so gradually, seldom appearing among the percentage leaders.

A familiarity with this particular table can be helpful, though, in keeping the fortunes of individual stocks in perspective. When you watch a $120 stock moving up or down $1 or $2 almost daily, you may feel a sense of volatility. A $12 stock, rising or falling an eighth or a quarter of a point, may seem relatively placid. But in fact, even small moves can translate into significant percentage profits or losses in lower-priced stocks. As a general rule, lower-priced issues tend to be more volatile than their high-priced counterparts.

CHAPTER FIVE

CORPORATE EARNINGS AND DIVIDEND REPORTS

So far, the 15-Minute Investor has been concentrating on the financial markets themselves and the individual securities traded in them. The next step broadens the scope, with a check in the newspaper's earnings and dividends tables for the latest results achieved by any companies you are following. Most companies issue reports quarterly, operating on a calendar fiscal year. So the flow of this information tends to reach flood stage in mid- to late January, April, July, and October. Dividends, which normally must be voted by companies' boards of directors, may or may not be announced at the same time that earnings are reported.

For one reason or another, a good many companies run their businesses on a fiscal year that does not coincide with the calendar. So almost every business day, there are at least a few earnings reports published. If you have a personal interest in following only a handful of companies, there will be many days when you may want to devote little or no time to the earnings tables. But once you become a practiced reader of them, you might want to scan them briefly even when none of your prime companies show up on the list. You could, for example, spot an unfamiliar name that shows a dramatic improvement from a year ago. This information, in and of itself, may be "old news" to the market, and quite likely will already have been reflected in the price of the company's stock. But you may nevertheless clip the item, or make a note of it, for further investigation. What business developments, you might want to inquire, have contributed to the higher earnings? Do they signal a trend that is likely to continue in future quarters (and future years, for that matter)?

In the abstract, earnings and dividends are what investing in stocks is all about. They represent the financial achievements of an enterprise in which you, as a shareholder, are part owner. Thus, casual observers of the markets are often puzzled when a stock goes nowhere, or even declines, after a company reports what look like impressive earnings results or increases its dividend.

These days, of course, the affairs of almost all large companies, and many smaller ones as well, are closely and continuously monitored by professional security analysts employed by brokerage houses, independent investment advisory services, and money management firms. One of their primary functions is to estimate what a given company will earn not only in the current quarter, but for all of the current year—and often the next year as well. Thus, the market's immediate reaction to an earnings report is quite often based on whether the figures exceed, match, or fall short of expectations. When Ultratech Medical Miracles Corp. posts a 25 percent earnings increase, and the stock falls 8¼ points, the explanation is frequently quite simple. Analysts had been projecting a gain of at least 35, 40, or 50 percent.

In an investment world dominated by institutions, whose hired managers compete fiercely with each other to show superior performance results, a single quarterly disappointment can send a stock into a tailspin for a few hours or even a few days. As an individual investor, you should be in a position to be more patient and less prone to panic. You need not play the game the way the institutions do, and indeed you probably lack the time and resources even to try.

With that sense of perspective in mind, you turn on a given day to the earnings tables and see a familiar name:

HYPOTHETICAL CORP.

Qtr to Dec. 30	1985	1984
Revenue $	91,070,000	88,840,000
Net inc	5,435,000	5,431,000
Share earns	.58	.58
Yr rev	309,660,000	264,132,000
Net inc	23,890,000	19,967,000
Share earns	2.54	2.19

For the full year, Hypothetical showed good gains in all respects, earning $23.89 million, or $2.54 per share, on sales of $309.66 million. A year earlier, its profits were slightly less than $20 million, or $2.19 a share, on sales of $264.13 million. The fourth quarter was not so good, however—earnings were little changed, or "flat" in Wall Street parlance, while sales increased slightly.

On the surface, that's troublesome news, worth checking into. The nice growth Hypothetical has been enjoying seems to have stalled. Still, like any earnings report, it needs to be put into the context of other information you have previously gathered. You already know that Hypothetical's stock rose half a point to 30½ in yesterday's trading, maintaining its price-earnings multiple at a respectable 12, and holding in the upper half of its trading range over the past fifty-two weeks. So the earnings either were reported after the market closed, or came as no disturbing surprise to Wall Street. A quick check with your broker or Hypothetical's investor relations department should tell you which of those two possibilities applies.

If you have been keeping tabs on Hypothetical for some time, you may recall reading several weeks previously that Hypothetical's management had forecast a flat quarter, with a resumption of earnings growth in the new year. All that having been said, however, you might be inclined to look at Hypothetical's investment merits a little more cautiously than before. Many a time, it seems, when a stream of good news from a growing company is interrupted by an adverse report, the first disappointment isn't the last.

Before leaving the matter of Hypothetical, you check the newspaper's dividend table, which is divided under several headings: Irregular, Stock, Initial, Increased, Reduced, Omitted, Regular, and so forth. In the "regular" section, you find

Hypothetical Corp.   Q   .25   2–10   2–28

Hypothetical, in its present business circumstances, has decided to keep its quarterly (as indicated by the "Q") dividend at the previously prevailing rate of $1 per share annually. The next payout will be to holders of record as of Feb. 10 (2–10), and will be distributed on Feb. 28. That means that should you sell your Hypothetical stock on, say, Feb. 18, you will still be entitled to receive the dividend distributed ten days later.

One further note on the subject of earnings, dividends, stock prices, and price-earnings ratios. In making any calculations using these data, it is good to bear in mind that some of the numbers are "hard," and others "soft." There is no arguing, for example, with yesterday's closing price of a stock, though many investors might like to. A cash dividend is an absolute money-in-the-pocket figure. But earnings are not such a firm number. To be sure, they're spelled out with painstaking precision, right down to the last penny per share. But corporate earnings are figured through a process somewhat like the one you go through when you fill out your tax return. At about every second or third flash of the calculator, a question of interpretation comes up. (Hoary Wall Street joke: "What are our earnings for the quarter, auditor?" the company president asks. "What do you want them to be?" auditor replies.) So whenever you set about building an edifice of elaborate calculations based on figures like price-earnings ratios, it makes sense to remember that the foundation of your structure is not necessarily concrete.

CHAPTER SIX

ECONOMIC STATISTICS, ANALYSES, AND INVESTMENT COLUMNS

The 15-Minute Investor now moves on from the subjects of the securities markets, individual securities, and corporate news to check the latest pulse readings of the economy at large. These don't come along every single day, but they are many and frequent: inflation and unemployment rates, gross national product, housing starts, money supply, leading indicators, and more.

As investment tools, economic statistics are notoriously imperfect. A number reported today may be inaccurate because of sampling bias, outdated assumptions about how the economy works, or simple mathematical error. Even if none of those problems arises, the figure may be substantially revised (and in practice many statistics routinely are) later on, when more information is available. Once a final figure is settled upon, its significance may be exaggerated or misinterpreted, or it may be too old to be of anything but historical use. The more dramatic a figure may be, the more likely it is that the government agency or private firm that calculated it will dismiss it as an aberration. In any case, everyone agrees, no single statistic covering a week, a month, or a quarter should ever be taken as firm evidence of a lasting trend.

Consider what Census Director John G. Keane, head of one of the world's biggest statistics-processing entities, had to say in the magazine *American Demographics:* "Despite centuries of statistical evolution, burgeoning computer technology, and an expanding educational emphasis on quantitative methods, people frequently abuse statistics. This abuse misleads an unwary public.''

Wall Street analysts criticize the press, with some justification, for overemphasizing, even sensationalizing, statistics that turn out to have a very short shelf life. The press criticizes politicians, again with some justification, for distorting data to support their own positions and make themselves look good. The issuers of statistics, for their part, regularly publish disclaimers along with their reports, pointing out the limitations of the data.

Yet just about every Wall Street house of any size seems to have a staff of highly trained experts who try to estimate government statistics in advance. Independent firms collect their projections, tabulate "consensus" forecasts, and publish them. The day before a government report (put together amid elaborate security procedures) is due out, rumors may sweep through Wall Street that it is going to contain bad/good news for bonds/stocks/both. When the figure is finally released, the markets may rally on the fact that it doesn't look as bad as investors had feared it might.

Who started this circus, and why does it go on and on and on? No complete answer is readily at hand. The best explanation seems to be that there is no appealing alternative. To simply let the economy roll along without trying to track its path certainly doesn't recommend itself. It can be agreed all around that each individual statistic should be treated as but one piece of a very big puzzle. But does that permit bond traders, competing against each other for every thirty-second of a dollar or every .01 of a point with huge amounts of their employers' capital, to sit back for a couple of weeks and let the whole picture form gradually in their minds?

On this point, the 15-Minute Investor's lack of access to up-to-the-minute data around the clock may be viewed as an advantage, rather than an obstacle. Away from the glaring video terminals and chattering news tickers, you may have the luxury of concentrating on what Wall Street analyst Raymond F.

DeVoe, Jr. calls "slow ideas"—the kind of subtle change that, seen in future retrospective, marks something of lasting importance. In DeVoe's analogy, you can try to spot the turn of the tide while others are jumping every wave.

In that spirit, the pages that follow contain capsule discussions of many of the periodic statistical reports that Wall Streeters watch each other watching. No attempt whatever has been made at mathematical (or any other kind of) sophistication. For greater detail on the systems and methods that go into calculating the numbers, you might wish to consult the government's *Handbook of Cyclical Indicators*. Copies are available from the U.S. Government Printing Office.

GROSS NATIONAL PRODUCT

The government's figures on GNP—economists almost always refer to it by those initials—attempt nothing less than to measure the total of all economic activity in this country. The Commerce Department, which reports GNP figures quarterly, defines it as "the market value of the goods and services produced by the labor and property supplied by residents of the United States." One way of figuring it is to add up the value of every purchase made in a given quarter, and then to adjust the sum upward or downward by whatever change occurred during the same period in business inventories of unsold goods. There are other ways which do not produce quite the same number ("a statistical discrepancy, which reflects measurement error," says the government), but no matter.

The lead paragraph in a news story about the latest GNP figure may simply state it this way: "The economy grew at a faster-than-expected 4.5 percent annual rate in the first three months of this year, the government reported Friday." If the GNP is taken as the single measure that most closely embodies overall economic activity, it is obviously worth investors' attention. Unfortunately, the figures refuse to sit still for long. In the last month of a quarter, the government issues its first projection of what GNP appears to have done over the three-month period. This "flash" estimate is obviously subject to later revision—at the time of its release the quarter isn't even over yet. Indeed, a few weeks later there comes a revised figure which is still described as "preliminary." It is subject to change again in future months, even as government statisticians have begun reporting early readings for subsequent quarters.

Since GNP is measured in dollars, it naturally tends to be distorted by inflation. Think of the whole output of the economy as a carton of one dozen large white Grade A eggs. If one of these cartons sold in 1980 for 89 cents, and an identical one sold in 1981 for 99 cents, the "output" of the economy might be stated to have increased by 11.2 percent, when in fact it has not changed at all. For that reason, most economists look at "real" GNP—total output adjusted to the 1972 purchasing power of the dollar. The unadjusted figure is known as "nominal" GNP. By the way, the government also discloses the inflation rate it calculates as part of the computation of real GNP. This is known as the GNP deflator, and some experts think it a better measure of inflation (though less timely) than the separate monthly government data on the consumer price index and producer price indexes.

The stock market typically responds strongly to GNP figures only when they come in significantly above or below private economists' advance estimates. In theory, the main concern of investors as a group is not what the economy is doing now, but the present forces that will shape its performance six months to a year from now.

It stands to reason that a strong GNP should make for a strong stock market. Yet it doesn't usually work out so simply. In recent years, big GNP numbers have tended to conjure up fears on Wall Street of an "overheating" economy—a growth rate that cannot be sustained for long before inflationary pressures increase, prompting the Federal Reserve to tighten, or restrict, the supply of money flowing through the economy, and thereby push interest rates higher. This chain of events presumably sets the stage for a slowing of GNP growth in the future, or even a recession, traditionally defined as a period in which real GNP declines for at least two consecutive quarters. A borderline case, in which GNP grows a little bit over a six-month period but unemployment increases, is sometimes given the oxymoronic label "growth recession."

Thus it happens that stock market investors often show a perverse preference for a small GNP increase rather than a big one. "Good news is bad news," runs the frequently repeated maxim on Wall Street, which goes a long way toward explaining why economics is called "the dismal science." The Street's most notorious lovers of bad news are traders in the bond market, where changing levels of interest rates call the tune for just about everything that happens.

UNEMPLOYMENT

Probably no single economic statistic carries a greater emotional charge than the Labor Department's monthly report on the unemployment rate—the percentage of Americans sixteen years of age and older who are considered to be members of the civilian (non-military) labor force but who do not have jobs. Other data, like GNP figures, may appear to be no more than hazy abstractions to the average citizen, while the desire to get and keep a job, and the fear of losing one, is a very real and personal matter. Employment is economics at its most human level.

So it contributes to the Scroogian image of Wall Street when the stock market seems to pay relatively little heed to the ups and downs of the unemployment rate. The fact is, though, that the rate itself usually tells investors little or nothing that would immediately alter their plans. It is a seasonally adjusted figure that is the product of many variables. It can rise even in a month when total employment increases, if government surveyors conclude that there has been an even greater expansion of the number of people in the labor force.

Furthermore, it is not considered a good indicator of future economic trends. If anything, job gains and losses tend to lag behind other economic developments. When the economy begins to emerge from a recession, for example, business managers may be slow to hire new workers because they are not yet confident that the worst is over, and because they are still very cost-conscious after the problems they have encountered during the business slump.

When the unemployment rate is announced each month, most Wall Street analysts quickly look past it to other data that accompany its release, such as overall employment, nonfarm payrolls, and the average work week. These numbers are thought to be better measurements of the state of the economy. The unemployment rate itself can occasionally cause a stir in the securities markets if its political significance appears so great that it might prompt some change in government policy. Otherwise, it is generally bigger news on the front page than in the business section.

Every now and then, bond traders find themselves in the unseemly position of appearing to rejoice over unexpected negative news on employment. However, if the employment figures paint a picture of unexpected weakness in the economy, it is only logical for them to conclude that interest rates should fall. Lower interest rates mean higher bond prices and, not incidentally, the prospect of a possible increase in employment some time in the future. Therefore, castigate not the bond traders for thriving like jackals on the misfortune of others. Like the rest of us, they are only doing (and trying to keep) their jobs.

THE MONEY SUPPLY

For about the past decade, a strange weekly ritual has been performed on Wall Street. After the close of the stock market on a Thursday or Friday afternoon, countless traders, brokers, economists, analysts, and just plain investors fix their eyes on financial news tickers, awaiting the Federal Reserve's report on the money supply. As they appear, the numbers are quickly scanned for their presumed implications for future monetary policy and interest rates, and feverish activity erupts in the credit markets.

If you are an investor with a long-term point of view, most students of the markets suggest that you pay this spectacle little mind. Money makes the economy and the markets go, they readily acknowledge, and changes in the supply of it are matters of great interest to investors. But as the Fed itself frequently points out, week-to-week fluctuations in a single measure of the money supply are no reliable sign of any important trends.

The figure that commands the most immediate attention on Wall Street is the "basic" money supply, or M1. It is a seasonally adjusted figure, subject to later revision, that represents the total amount of cash in circulation in the economy, plus outstanding travelers checks and deposits in checking accounts. That is just one of many possible ways to define "money," however. Take M1, add in a few other things like certain savings deposits and assets of money market mutual funds, and you have M2. Or put cash in circulation together with the reserves that banks and other financial institutions have on deposit with the Fed, and you get what is known as the monetary base.

There are numerous other yardsticks, but none of them seems up to the job of pinning the subject down precisely. When you count up the spendable money available to Americans, shouldn't you also consider the money they have in stocks, bonds, and mutual funds? If you do, you must consider that should everyone try to spend that money at once, a lot of it would simply vanish.

With all these difficulties, most analysts agree that intermediate to long-term trends in the money supply are of great importance to the markets. If monetary growth is too slow, business activity may well suffer, along with demand for securities like stocks and bonds. If the money supply expands too fast, by contrast, it may increase inflationary pressures and expectations (in the parlance of economics, "too many dollars chasing too few goods"). The problem, of course, is determining how slow is too slow, and how fast is too fast. The Fed periodically sets, and reports to Congress and the public, target minimum and maximum growth rates for the principal monetary measures over given periods of time. When growth strays outside this target range, however, the Fed does not necessarily respond with a change in its credit policy right away. At times, it has been known simply to proclaim a new set of targets.

THE CONSUMER
PRICE INDEX

The CPI is the best known measure of inflation trends in this country. It is reported monthly by the Labor Department's Bureau of Labor Statistics, and Wall Street economists watch it closely. In compiling the index, which uses 1967 prices as a base level of 100, government researchers check prices paid by urban wage earners for hundreds of items ranging from haircuts to houses.

Thorough as it may be, the CPI cannot precisely measure any individual family's experience with the cost of living. You may buy a car every two years, or you may not own one at all. Furthermore, Social Security and income taxes, which have been a rising cost for many Americans over most of this century, are not included in the index.

A further drawback of the CPI for investors is that it measures present price conditions without providing much information about the future course of inflation. For signs of what the future might hold, investment professionals are generally inclined to look elsewhere—at the money supply, at commodity price indexes and sensitive individual commodities like gold, and to some extent at the producer price indexes.

PRODUCER PRICE
INDEXES

These indexes, like the CPI, are reported monthly, with a base of 1967 prices equal to 100. Separate indexes are calculated for items at various stages of the production process—for instance, crude materials for further processing; intermediate materials, supplies, and components; and finished consumer goods. All told, data is collected on about 2,800 items that come from agriculture, forestry, fishing, mining, manufacturing, and utilities.

The producer price index that gets the most attention in the press and on Wall Street is the one for finished goods. It measures price levels at what amounts to the next-to-last stop in the production and distribution process, before goods reach the shelves of retail stores and are priced for sale to consumers. As such, it can be used by investors as an indication of where consumer prices might be headed in the near to intermediate future.

INDEX OF
LEADING ECONOMIC
INDICATORS

Since so many people, investors included, are more interested in the future of the economy than its past or present state, the government publishes a monthly index designed to function as a kind of economic crystal ball. It has twelve components:

- The average weekly hours worked by production workers and other nonsupervisory employees in manufacturing
- The average number of initial claims filed for state unemployment insurance
- New orders received, adjusted for inflation, by manufacturers in the consumer goods and materials industries
- "Vendor performance," that is, the percentage of companies reporting a slowing of deliveries for items they have ordered
- An index of the net number of businesses being formed
- The number of contracts signed and orders placed for new production facilities such as plants and equipment
- An index of building permits approved by local authorities for construction of new private housing units

- The inflation-adjusted change in manufacturing and trade inventories
- The change in price of selected "sensitive" raw materials
- The month-to-month change in the average level of Standard & Poor's 500-stock composite index
- The inflation-adjusted change in the M2 measure of the money supply
- The increase or decrease in the amount of consumer and business credit outstanding.

Each of these items represents a business or financial event that has some logical predictive value. A slowdown in deliveries, for instance, is a sign that suppliers are having trouble keeping pace with orders they are receiving. It hints strongly at an impending increase in production to meet demand. Unemployment claims, by contrast, are a negative leading indicator if they increase.

Perhaps the most intriguing of the twelve indicators is stock prices. Naturally, a rising stock market tends to increase the wealth of shareowners, at least on paper, and along with it their confidence, sense of prosperity, and willingness to spend. Beyond that, the stock market has gained a reputation as a good, if less than perfect, predictor of the economy. On a large scale, the market serves as a sort of public opinion poll that measures how the investing public feels not by what it may say, but by what it does with its money. Indeed, some analysts argue that the market is the best leading indicator of all.

That poses a problem for investors, however. How can they use the index of leading indicators, which in part represents the *past performance* of stocks, as any sort of guide to what the market might do in the future? Some investment analysts argue that they can't get much benefit from it.

In practice, the index has a somewhat erratic record. Experience has shown that a single month's reading, no matter how dramatically changed from the previous month, is unlikely to be a reliable guide. Over the years a rough rule of thumb has evolved on Wall Street: When the index changes direction and rises or falls for three consecutive months, it is time to give it some serious consideration. Even when the index makes a correct "call," its timing can vary widely. The change it signals in the business climate may be close at hand or still many months away.

As you glanced through the list of the index's components, perhaps a couple of them struck you as a bit equivocal. An increase in prices of sensitive raw materials may be "good" in the sense that it serves as an early-warning signal of a potential increase in production demand. But might it not also suggest that inflationary pressures are picking up? The same might also be said for an increase in the money supply.

When all the limitations are considered, some Wall Street analysts still pay a good deal of attention to the leading indicators. Others minimize its importance. Still others who are unsatisfied with the leading indicators watch other indexes, published at the same time, of "coincident" and "lagging" indicators. A ratio of the coincident to lagging indicators, they maintain, has a better forecasting record than the leading indicators themselves.

INDUSTRIAL
PRODUCTION

This index, reported monthly by the Federal Reserve Board, measures the output of the nation's manufacturers, mining companies, and electric and natural gas utilities. By its very makeup, it serves as a gauge of the health of "smokestack America." For the past few decades, manufacturing in this country has endured many problems, including intensified competition from abroad. The most dynamic growth in the U.S. economy has occurred elsewhere, most notably in service industries ranging from advertising and health care to security and building maintenance.

Industrial production, then, is not an all-encompassing measure in a league with the gross national product. Aside from the service economy, it omits farming, construction, transportation, and retail and wholesale trade. Nevertheless, many analysts believe it remains an important vital sign of the economy. If industrial production is weak for a prolonged period, they argue, demand will most likely suffer sooner or later in the other sectors as well.

NEW ORDERS FOR DURABLE GOODS

The Commerce Department reports monthly on the total value of new orders received by manufacturers of durable goods—products with a normal life of at least three years. Orders for durable goods are regarded as especially significant because their purchase, or at least the timing of it, is often discretionary. In the case of a family, the budget for nondurables such as food may be fairly constant, in good times or bad. The same family is most likely to buy a new car or furniture when it is feeling most prosperous. The same goes for businesses that, while consuming fairly steady amounts of paper clips and electricity, may vary greatly their spending for durables like transportation equipment and machinery.

The figures for any given month, it should be noted, can be skewed by wide fluctuations in orders from the Defense Department. Many Wall Street analysts make a practice of checking the accompanying report of new orders for "nondefense capital goods." The level of capital spending tells a good deal about business managers' confidence and their willingness to spend for long-term projects that theoretically increase productivity and provide new avenues for growth.

From a cyclical standpoint, capital spending traditionally peaks in the latter stages of a period of economic expansion, when business conditions are at their best, and confidence is high all around. Veterans of the stock market wars point out that bull markets often top out in circumstances like these. Capital spending is a central element in the economy, and it contributes significantly to the overall level of business activity and prosperity. However, the evidence of the past suggests the increasing capital spending amounts to something less than a clarion call for investors to buy stocks.

HOUSING STARTS

If capital spending usually hits its peak late in a period of economic expansion, housing starts often tell quite a different story. Because their ups and downs are closely linked to interest-rate trends, housing may be the first sector of the economy to show signs of a revival after a recession. The Commerce Department issues a monthly report on the number of housing units for which construction has been begun. The figure is seasonally adjusted since weather, among other calendar variables, has a significant effect on building activity. Even with seasonal adjustment, housing starts figures can be very volatile from month to month.

Along with housing starts, the government reports monthly on an index of permits granted by local authorities for new construction. Since permits may be issued several weeks or months before actual building begins, many Wall Street analysts look to the permits figure as a forward indicator of building activity. In a few cases, government researchers note, builders change their plans and do not act on permits they have been given.

Housing data merits investors' attention for several reasons. The construction industry is a significant part of the economy in its own right. In addition, home building plays an important role in determining the fortunes of many other industries, including those that produce building materials like lumber and cement, and those that make home furnishings such as appliances and furniture. Because the pace of homebuilding is closely linked to the supply and cost of credit, investors who have an interest in the construction industries keep a close watch on present and possible future trends in interest rates.

RETAIL SALES AND
THE CONSUMER

Investors have several ways of monitoring retail sales and, by implication, the status of consumer spending which, in its broadest definition, accounts for as much as two-thirds of economic activity in this country. The Commerce Department reports a monthly retail sales figure that is adjusted for seasonal variations (sales tend to be strongest in the Christmas selling season and, to a lesser extent, at other special points of the year such as Easter and the back-to-school season). Large individual retailers also make monthly sales reports, which are analyzed in roundup stories published by most newspapers. Auto manufacturers report on domestic car sales every ten days, and their figures are also covered in regular news stories.

Commerce also tracks and reports monthly on personal income—defined as money received by individuals from their jobs and other sources such as interest, dividends, and payments from transfer programs like Social Security and unemployment insurance—and personal spending, for most goods and services except homes. Separately, the Federal Reserve Board provides seasonally adjusted data on the amount of consumer credit outstanding. This figure includes individuals' outstanding debt on short- and intermediate-term loans from financial institutions, and on credit cards. It does not include loans for business purposes or home mortgages.

The view Wall Street analysts take of the latest consumer credit numbers usually depends on the prevailing state of the economy. In a situation in which the economy has been sluggish and consumers have been acting cautiously, a large increase in consumer credit may be seen as a welcome sign of revived confidence and improving business conditions. On the other hand, an expansion of consumer credit at a time when the economy is already booming may be taken as a warning signal that debt is growing excessively.

Some private organizations—including the University of Michigan's Survey Research Center and the Conference Board, an independent business research organization—compile indexes of consumer sentiment that receive some attention on Wall Street. Despite this abundance of information, the American consumer remains a highly unpredictable beast, as anyone in the business of setting government policies or producing and marketing goods for public consumption will readily attest.

CAPACITY UTILIZATION

The Federal Reserve Board publishes a monthly calculation of the extent to which manufacturers are using their available production facilities. The maximum possible (or "capacity") output is defined as "the level of output that can be achieved during a given period with existing plant and equipment and a normal operating schedule." Actual output is reported as a percentage of capacity output.

Ideally, one might think, production should be as close to peak capacity as possible. That would logically be the most productive use of capital invested in production facilities. In practice, however, when output gets close to capacity it begins to cause problems. At or near capacity, additional orders may be difficult to fill without significant extra costs for things like overtime pay. Shortages can occur in spots, with supply problems most likely for those goods and materials that are most in demand. Extra costs and shortages naturally lead toward price increases (and inflation).

Of course, high capacity utilization rates also act as a spur to new investment in plants and equipment. By an old Wall Street rule of thumb, this becomes a significant force when the utilization rate gets to about 85 percent. A very low rate of capacity utilization signals an economy with significant problems. Rapid changes in technology can have a significant effect on utilization of existing capacity, by making yesterday's productive plants and equipment obsolete or difficult to operate at an attractive rate of financial return.

CORPORATE PROFITS

The Commerce Department makes a quarterly report on after-tax corporate profits, adjusted for seasonal factors. Overall business profitability is without question a significant factor in the health of the economy. But by the time this report goes out, Wall Street generally has already formed a pretty clear impression of the trend in corporate profits. Many investors, naturally, have a greater interest in the earnings figures posted separately by individual companies whose stocks are traded in the market.

FOREIGN TRADE

A healthy flow of goods and services in and out of this country through international markets is of great importance to the health and well-being of the domestic economy. Imports make available to American consumers a wide array of items at prices below what they would cost if they were produced at home. Some important commodities are available largely, or only, from overseas producers. At the same time, export sales play an important part in determining the degree of prosperity in major sectors of the U.S. economy such as agriculture and manufacturing.

The government compiles monthly figures on exports and imports. If exports exceed imports, the nation has a trade surplus. If imports exceed exports, it is said to have a trade deficit. The problem facing the United States lately has been a large deficit, which has been blamed primarily on the high value of the dollar in foreign exchange. When the dollar is strong against foreign currencies, it reduces the effective price U.S. consumers must pay for imports, and simultaneously raises the cost of American-made items to buyers overseas.

Matters of world trade and currency exchange can be enormously complicated, both politically and economically. In the past decade, some of our trade partners have complained both when the dollar was low in value and when it was high. In recent years there has been much debate taking place over what to do about the country's trade imbalance. About the only point on which most analysts agreed was that a chronic deficit was troublesome and undesirable.

Investors with an interest in U.S. companies that do a large international business watch the ups and downs of the dollar in foreign-exchange trading, as well as the figures on the balance of trade, for developments that might affect the fortunes of those companies. With all the concern that it evoked, a wide trade deficit did not prevent the U.S. stock market from reaching record highs in 1985.

PURCHASING
MANAGERS SURVEY

Once a month, a trade group known as the National Association of Purchasing Management surveys its members for information on business conditions and prices. Newspaper reports of the results, issued on the first Monday of the month, contain commentary from officials of the association as well as statistics. Many stock market analysts and active investors make this part of their regular reading.

If you are an avid follower of all these and other periodic statistical reports on the state of the economy, you may want to know in advance when they are scheduled to be reported. Many large brokerage firms, and some financial and general interest newspapers, now publish weekly or monthly lists of forthcoming indicators. No matter how closely you follow them, they provide no guarantee of investment success. But at least they can help you stay tuned to the same frequency as full-time professional investors.

OTHER PERTINENT
REPORTS

Beyond economic statistics, there are many specialized announcements and disclosures that have a bearing on the securities markets. These include changes in "administered" interest rates that are not set entirely by market forces—for instance, the Federal Reserve's discount rate and commercial banks' prime lending rate. Reports from the mutual fund industry may reveal significant changes in the flow of large amounts of investment money. Stock exchanges issue monthly reports on short-selling activity, which many investors watch for possible effects on the market as a whole or on individual stocks they own or are monitoring.

The *prime rate* is a benchmark interest rate that represents, at least in theory, the charge imposed on loans to the biggest and most creditworthy customers of a bank or other lending institution. Changes in the prime do not come according to any set schedule, but are made at the discretion of individual banks as their own cost of money rises and falls in line with open-market interest rates.

In some instances, one or a few banks may raise or lower the prime, while other institutions hold to the old prevailing rate for several days or even weeks. At other times, a leading bank's move on the prime will be matched within a few hours by most or all of the industry. A few smaller banks across the country are especially aggressive in announcing cuts in their prime rates, with the unabashed motive of attracting favorable publicity.

The prime rate is usually a lagging, rather than a leading, indicator of trends in interest rates generally. By the time banks raise or lower the prime, the increase or decrease in open-market interest rates that prompted their decision is often widely recognized on Wall Street. But "old news" or not, a change in the prime most often is heralded by large headlines in the press, and it can have a marked short-term impact on stock and bond prices. Analysts say this may be partly psychological—a change in the prime can serve to put an ''official'' stamp on recent interest-rate trends. It also may have a real and immediate impact on the borrowing costs incurred by businesses and other bank borrowers. Whether a given company qualifies for borrowing at the prime rate, or must pay prime plus 3 percent, its cost of carrying bank debt rises and falls as the prime rate goes up and down.

Federal funds are overnight loans between banks. The interest rate on this money fluctuates constantly, and is reported daily by many newspapers. It may be influenced by operations of the Federal Reserve, and accordingly is closely watched by investment professionals looking for signs of the direction of, and any change in, the Fed's credit policy.

The discount rate. Banks and other financial institutions may also borrow short term from the Federal Reserve, through what is called the ''discount window.'' The interest rate on these loans, the discount rate, is set absolutely by the Fed. The discount rate, like the prime rate, is often described as a lagging rate that is usually changed in reaction to previous movements of other interest rates. Yet, perversely, the Fed quite often uses an increase or decrease in the discount rate when it wants to send out a strong signal of its desire to either tighten or relax its credit policy. Some analysts regard a sequence of three consecutive reductions in the discount rate as a strongly favorable portent for the stock market and, by similar reasoning, two or three discount-rate increases in a row as a distinct negative for stocks.

Treasury auctions. In order to finance the federal government's huge needs for money, the Treasury is a regular and heavy borrower. It holds weekly auctions of three- and six-month Treasury bills, monthly sales of one-year bills and two-year notes, quarterly ''refundings'' in which it sells longer-term notes and bonds, and sometimes supplemental offerings of some of these securities as circumstances warrant. The results of all these auctions are reported in most newspapers. Whenever the government puts a large new supply of its interest-bearing securities on the market, many analysts and investors watch the reception it receives closely for possible signs of the future direction of interest rates.

Strong demand, or competitive bidding at lower-than-expected interest rates, is naturally taken as a favorable sign. An unenthusiastic response is usually interpreted as evidence that interest rates must rise to bring supply and demand for debt securities back into balance. As long as the deficit between the government's spending and revenues remains wide, Treasury auctions promise to continue as a major force affecting the credit markets and, by extension, the stock market.

Margin requirements. The Federal Reserve is empowered to set, and change, the amount of initial deposit investors make when they buy stocks on margin—that is, using money borrowed from their brokers. From 1974 to the time this book was written, this minimum stood at 50 percent of the total purchase price. Of late, some Fed officials have talked of lowering margin requirements or even of deregulating this type of investment activity. Minimum margins are much lower for bonds than for stocks.

A relaxation of margin requirements could serve as a strong stimulus to buying of stocks by speculatively inclined investors. At the extreme, some analysts worry, it could lead to too much of a good thing. Most chroniclers agree that excessive margin speculation played a central role in the Great Crash of 1929. Still, it is generally believed that a change in margin requirements today would have less impact on the stock market than it might have had a couple of decades ago. Pension funds, the biggest participants in today's market, do not invest on margin at all. Furthermore, the past few years have seen dramatic growth in other, highly leveraged ways of speculating on the ups and downs of stock prices—futures and options on stock indexes, to name two of the most obvious examples.

Short interest. Each month the major stock exchanges issue reports on outstanding short positions for individual stocks traded in their markets, and for the sum of all those markets. A short position is created when an investor borrows stock from a broker and sells it, hoping to profit from an ensuing decline in the price of the stock involved. Since all short sales must sooner or later be "covered" by buying the stock back for return to the lending broker, short interest has traditionally been thought of as an indication of assured future demand for a stock.

That principle still applies, but to a lesser extent than it once did. In today's markets, many short sales are merely part of complex transactions in which traders take a "hedged" position. For instance, when they short a stock, they may at the same time buy call options giving them the right to buy an equal amount of shares at a specified price. Unlike other short sellers, traders with hedged positions cannot be caught in a "short squeeze," or panic to buy back stock at almost any price, for as long as their call options remain in effect.

Another measure of short sales, those made by traders in "odd lots" of less than 100 shares, is reported daily. It used to be considered wise strategy to monitor this activity closely, on the theory that small investors dealing in odd lots are usually wrong about the market at important turning points. Heavy odd-lot shorting was therefore considered a signal that stocks might be due for a rally. However valuable a tool this might have been in the past, it is less useful now because small investors have other ways to try to profit from market declines—for example, by buying put options that give them the right to sell a given stock at a specified price for a set period of time.

Mutual fund reports. The Investment Company Institute publishes a monthly report on money flows in and out of mutual funds and on the investment activities of the funds' managers. The institute, the fund industry's largest trade group, also issues weekly data on the assets of money market mutual funds and the net change in the total from the previous week.

When sales of new mutual fund shares to investors significantly exceed redemptions of existing shares, it is normally taken as evidence of public enthusiasm about the outlook for the investment markets. Beyond that, when new money flows into mutual funds, fund managers must do something to put it to work. So robust mutual fund sales are sometimes interpreted as a bullish portent for the stock market. However, it should be borne in mind that much of today's activity in mutual funds involves funds that do not participate in the stock market, but instead buy securities like government or municipal bonds.

In the monthly ICI report, some investors concentrate on the section that shows the percentage of stock mutual fund assets that are held in "cash," or short-term money market vehicles. When the cash ratio is high, it may be viewed as a large pool of potential future demand for stocks. When it is low, the funds effectively have expended much of their ammunition and, in theory at least, lack the firepower to contribute to any market rally in the near future.

With the great growth of money market mutual funds since they first began to appear in the early 1970s, Wall Street has come to monitor changes, week by week and over longer periods of time, in the total assets of these funds. Some of this money, after all, is held in brokerage firm central assets accounts that are maintained by active investors. So it would seem to be money that could move in the future into stocks, bonds, or both. Nevertheless, experience to date has shown that a lot of cash in money funds is "savings account" money as opposed to "investment" money. It tends to stay put, even in periods when interest rates fall sharply.

The 15-Minute Investor's check of pertinent economic and financial reports is complete. Next on the agenda come any news analyses covering the economic and political outlook, and any columns carried by the newspaper on investment subjects. By definition, these differ greatly from a lot of the "objective" data you have been gathering. Viewed in that light, they can help you to increase your knowledge and awareness of what is taking place in the markets.

Among newspapers with a national audience, the *Wall Street Journal* has its "Heard on the Street" column. The *New York Times* carries "Market Place." *USA Today* and *Investor's Daily* carry numerous stories focusing on separate stock groups and specialized investment subjects. In many other newspapers, the financial editor or columnist provides timely commentary on matters of investment interest, in particular focusing on companies and industries that are important to the local or regional economy. Several syndicated columnists who write on investing and personal finance have a national following. In addition to providing a wide range of business and financial news and tables, the Associated Press distributes several columns to its member newspapers. Among them are "Business Mirror," written five times a week primarily for afternoon newspapers, and the once-a-week "Weekly Wall Street," "Weekly Bonds," "Ticker Talk," and "On the Money."

Some investment columns are controversial at times. Wall Street professionals have been known to criticize them in certain cases as arbitrary and capricious "gossip columns." R. Foster Winans, a *Wall Street Journal* reporter who worked on "Heard on the Street" for a time in the early 1980s, was fired by the paper and criminally prosecuted on charges that he passed information about certain columns before their publication to friends for the purpose of trading on that information.

But aside from glaring exceptions like that one, most investment columns are written by conscientious people following strict ethical standards set by themselves and their employers. If they are provocative at times, well, part of their purpose is to give expression to the emotional as well as the calculating and analytical aspects of the struggle for investment success. At their best, they can also give their readers insights into the way successful analysts and investors play the game. They can add an important dimension to the statistical information that forms the basis of most investment decisions.

CHAPTER SEVEN

FREELANCING

In this last stage of your 15-minute review, the methodical, disciplined approach you have been following is abandoned. As the word freelancing implies, you are no longer deliberately tracking down a specific prey, but rather foraging for whatever of value you might come upon. A natural place to start is among the short news items buried below the day's main business and financial stories.

Perhaps a manufacturing company has closed one of its production facilities permanently. On the surface, this may look like just another symptom of an ailing business. On closer examination, it could turn out that the company has taken an important step toward cutting costs, ridding itself of operations that were a drag on its overall performance.

The search need not be confined to the business section. Trends and changing tastes and habits reported on the "living" or "lifestyle" pages may invite you to infer possible investment opportunities. A rate case story about an electric utility, published in the main news section, may tell you something about a change in your state's political climate that is either favorable or unfavorable for the company's outlook.

Beyond a few illustrative examples, the 15-Minute Investor's freelancing phase does not lend itself to detailed explication. It depends on spontaneity, curiosity, and imagination—assets you brought to the job of managing your money before you ever bought a stock or read your first investment book.

PART

II

BEYOND THE DAILY NEWS

The first part of this book outlined a system for monitoring your investments, the markets, and the economy on a regular basis—daily, or at least weekly. It is designed to take care of the regular routine of keeping informed. But obviously, following this system is not the only research and information-gathering the 15-Minute Investor will want or need to do. Some additional endeavors will arise according to a regular schedule—for example, once a year with the issuance of the annual report by a company whose stock you own. Others will arise irregularly and unpredictably, such as when you encounter a tidbit of news while freelancing in the daily paper that whets your appetite for more information.

A lot of successful investors keep their eyes and ears open constantly for investment ideas. There is no need to be obsessive about this, just alert and always ready to consider a given situation from an investment point of view.

In this section of the book, some of the most common information-gathering possibilities that are open to investors will be discussed, along with the benefits and perils that each may present. They won't by any means make you an overnight expert in corporate finance. But they will give you a start toward learning how to use your time to your financial benefit on those occasions when you have more than 15 minutes to work with.

ANNUAL REPORTS

All companies whose stocks are traded publicly in the United States are required to publish annual reports to their shareholders, providing certain basic information about their operations and results. At most companies, the preparation of this document goes far beyond the minimum effort required. Large amounts of hard work and money are lavished on reports that seem intended to serve as an eternal monument to the company, its top executives and staff, and its contributions to the world's well-being as well as to the wealth of its shareowners.

Annual reports have been the butt of so much criticism for so long that it seems pointless to dwell on their faults for very long here. It is presumed that as an intelligent 15-Minute Investor you can gaze at the glossy pictures and wade through the orotund prose without being dazzled and awed. True, most of the information in the annual report is very old news by the time it reaches your mailbox. But that doesn't mean it should be idly glanced at and then pitched in the wastebasket.

Even though much of it may be boring, in fact, why not read the whole thing? Yes, even look at the ostensibly useless photographs, and ask yourself what they tell you about the company's personality—how it sees itself, and the image it apparently wants to present to the world. Then turn to the chairman's letter and read it. It may be relentlessly upbeat, unspecific and tedious, but read it closely anyway to see if there might be some unexpected information presented either directly or between the lines.

Consider the actual case of a young, fast-growing company with many fans on Wall Street. In the company's 1984 annual report, its chairman and president said in the letter to shareholders:

> 1985 and 1986 will be years of transition. . . . We have grown rapidly; the most rapid growth among our pri-

mary competitors by a wide margin. Four years ago, we were little more than an idea; in 1985, we will approach $500 million in revenues.

In the past, the company's growth in profitability has largely been driven by its revenue growth, along with many of the more obvious approaches to reducing costs. During this period of transition, the company's focus will increasingly turn to further and continued improvement in the cost structure of our organization, and to putting in place the system and management to continue improving our control and margins. . . . improvements in control and reporting systems are imperative if we are to continue as a much larger company our historical pattern of earnings growth.

Not long afterward, the company surprised Wall Street by reporting that its earnings for the second quarter of 1985 would show no increase over the comparable period in 1984. It was the first time it failed to post a quarterly earnings gain since the company began to show profits more than three years earlier, and the stock ran into a spell of selling. The main difficulty, the company said, was cost-control problems at a couple of its operations. To a close reader of the letter in the annual report, that news might not have come as a totally unexpected development.

At the back of the typical annual report, you will find the financial statements, including the balance sheet (analogous to an individual's statement of net worth) and the income statement (roughly analogous to an individual's checking and other bank statements) for the year. The most important aspects of this information usually have been reported previously. Beyond that, there is an art to reading financial statements, and developing skill in doing so requires some time and practice. A good way to start acquiring this skill is to obtain a guide such as "How to Read a Financial Report," published by Merrill Lynch, Pierce, Fenner & Smith.

Once you have checked the numbers, financial experts routinely counsel, there are two additional items not to be overlooked: the report of the company's independent accountants, and the footnotes to the financial statements. The accountants' report usually consists of two paragraphs which state, in effect, that the auditors have checked to see that the figures are bona fide, and that they did so using methods that are "generally accepted" in the accounting profession. Any "howevers," "excepts," or other qualifying declarations in the accountants' report are likely to be red flags that merit your close attention and further investigation.

Though they might give the impression of being incidental, the footnotes to the financial statements may well contain some of the most important information in the entire report, whether it pertains to some litigation involving the company, some change in its financial procedures, or any number of other possible matters of great concern.

"Most people do not like to read footnotes because they may be complicated and they are almost always hard to read," says Merrill Lynch in its booklet. "That's too bad, because footnotes sometimes can be dynamite. And even if they don't reveal that the corporation has been forced into bankruptcy, footnotes can still tell you many fascinating sidelights on the financial story."

ANNUAL MEETINGS

In principle, the annual meeting is the ultimate exercise in corporate democracy. It provides the shareholders with a chance to vote for or against many actions the company's management proposes to take, on matters both mundane and significant. It can serve as a forum for dissident shareholders to try to make radical changes in the way things are done, whether they want to stop the company from polluting the environment or to force out the people who are now running the show. Some full-time "activist" shareholders have made names for themselves with their gadfly presence at annual meetings. And after the business on the agenda has been taken care of, top executives are often available to answer questions from even the smallest shareholder.

Often, management will have some announcement to make at the annual meeting, such as an estimate of the next quarter's earnings, if only to try to make it a newsworthy event. But is it worth the time, trouble, and expense for a small shareholder to attend annual meetings, especially those held far from the investor's home? The answer to that depends in large part on your own personal inclinations, and the time and travel money you have at your disposal.

You can, of course, vote on matters presented at the annual meeting without attending in person, using the mail proxy statements provided in advance (more about them shortly). Reporters from newspapers and financial publications cover many annual meetings, especially those of large companies and those of particular interest in the area where you live. So if there is any dramatic news made, you can learn of it without having been there to hear it yourself.

As in political elections, you may tell yourself that you ought to attend as many pertinent annual meetings as possible, to make your presence felt and to help, in however small a way, to see that the system operates the way it is supposed to. On the other hand, consider the views expressed by 272 "top investment professionals" surveyed by the Financial Relations Board Inc., a New York public relations firm, in 1985.

"With the 1985 annual meeting season over, many investment professionals surveyed place little value on that event in their stock appraisal process," the firm reported. "Over a third said they attended no annual meetings at all this year, and another 15 percent said they attended only one. Some 42 percent said they attended two to six of the events, and about 10 percent attended more than six.

"However, almost two thirds of the respondents said that

they would attend more of these meetings if companies would present more detailed business plan and outlook data instead of rehashing what happened last year."

PROSPECTUSES

The securities laws and rules require that any offering of new securities to the public must be made by means of a prospectus that describes the offering company's condition and what it plans to do with the money being raised. If you find annual reports tough sledding, wait until you get a gander at the legal boiler-plate and other dense prose contained in many of these documents. Prospectuses don't even have any pretty pictures to relieve the monotony.

In fairness, it must be said that some considerable efforts have been made in recent years to make prospectuses more readable and understandable. Easy to read or not, prospectuses almost always contain vital information that should be absorbed before you commit your money.

In the case of an offering of stock or other securities, the actual sale is preceded by a preliminary prospectus—known as a "red herring" because of the statement, printed in red ink on its cover, that a registration statement has been filed with the Securities and Exchange Commission, but has not yet become effective. Presumably, the allusion to the other meaning of "red herring" (a false clue or other distraction meant to put blood-hounds off the scent) is entirely tongue-in-cheek.

The prospectus normally contains financial information about the company involved, much as it would appear in an annual report, as well as a discussion of the company's history and prospects. One section that gets especially close scrutiny from experienced investors is the one headed "risk factors" or "special considerations." One prospectus, issued by a New York savings bank planning to convert from depositor to stockholder ownership, cautioned, "The shares of common stock being offered are not savings accounts or deposits and are not insured by the Federal Deposit Insurance Corp. or any other government agency.''

That might seem a pretty elementary point to any experienced investor. Yet it is very likely that many of the bank's depositors who were contemplating the possibility of investing in the bank in its new form were uncertain of the distinction. Many more startling disclosures have appeared in prospectuses of new ventures seeking to raise money from the public—for example, that while the company had an idea for a new product, it had not yet manufactured any of it and had no customers as yet.

In the case of mutual funds, the prospectus is a continuing document that is normally issued in updated form at least once a year, since mutual funds stand ready to sell new shares at any time. A mutual fund prospectus contains much information of primary interest to would-be investors, as seen in this list compiled by the United Mutual Fund Selector, an advisory letter:

- Minimum initial and subsequent minimum investments
- Statement of objective (growth, income, etc.)
- Investment methods (types of securities owned, limitations on strategies such as borrowing money or selling short)
- How to buy and redeem shares, and any charges imposed up front or on redemption
- Management background and fees
- Special services offered, such as retirement accounts and switching privileges with other funds
- Financial data and performance record.

PROXY STATEMENTS
AND OTHER
DISCLOSURE DOCUMENTS

The primary purpose of proxy statements is to provide shareholders with a convenient means of casting their votes on matters affecting corporations in which they own shares. The statement normally includes a ballot on which you can mark your choices and authorize a party present at a shareholder meeting to act as your proxy, or representative, by casting your vote for you. On some routine matters, such as the authorization of an increase in the number of shares to permit a stock split, returning the ballot may seem nothing more than a troublesome formality. However, many corporations stress the importance of going to the trouble so that votes may be cast without the expense of multiple mailings and telephone solicitations.

On other occasions, the proxy statement may be anything but a routine matter. If a dissident shareholder group seeks to oust present directors and management, or is pushing for some other major change in a company, you may receive statements from both sides in a proxy fight. The outcome of such a battle can be expected to have a material impact on the price of the stock you own, and thus the whole affair merits your close attention and study.

Whether they come to you amid calm or controversy, proxy statements may contain information of great interest that is readily available nowhere else. For example, one may tell you how many shares of the enterprise are owned by directors and senior managers. The proxy statement of a mutual fund you own may well strike you as cause for concern if it shows that many board members have only token stakes in the fund.

The proxy statement may also report on the latest year's compensation, including bonuses, received by top managers. This is worthy of your attention if only because these people are supposed to be working for you, as well as for themselves. If a company's earnings and stock price are low, but the top executives are taking home big bonuses, you may well have cause to ask some questions and raise some objections. Of course, it is not sensible to expect top management to work for very low pay either, except in extraordinary circumstances. In a paper published by the National Bureau of Economic Research, Sherwin Rosen, an economics professor at the University of Chicago, argued that top managers' pay must be disproportionately high to allow the competitive system of advancement to work to best advantage.

Rosen noted that in men's professional tennis tournaments, more than half the total prize money is typically allotted to the top four finishers. "Concentration is less extreme in the executive labor market," he wrote. "But nonetheless, those attaining top-ranking positions receive more than proportionate shares of compensation. In career games workers have many rungs in the hierarchical ladder to aspire to in the early stages of their careers, and this plays an important role in maintaining their enthusiasm for continuing. But the further one has climbed, the fewer the rungs left to attain. If top prizes are not large enough, those who have succeeded in attaining high ranks rest on their laurels and slack off in their efforts to climb higher."

Another disclosure document perused closely by many avid investors is the 10K, a form filed annually by corporations with the Securities and Exchange Commission that often contains information not published in the annual report. Generally, companies do not send copies of the 10K to individual investors as a matter of routine. But you should be able to obtain one through a broker, or by writing or telephoning the company's top financial officer or its investor relations department.

The first word of a change in a company's situation or condition may come in any of several other disclosure documents—possibly in a quarterly report to shareholders, which generally contains unaudited operating results for the latest fiscal quarter; or in filings made by the company in connection with its plans to offer some new issue of securities. Probably the best way to watch for developments like these is to be a regular and alert reader of a newspaper or other publication that does a good job of covering companies of interest to you.

THE BUSINESS PRESS

Most successful investors are avid readers of business information. Their reading, naturally, starts with the daily newspaper, but it does not stop there. Professional analysts on Wall Street often read not only general business magazines, but also trade publications covering the industries they follow. It may require considerable time and expense, but if you are so inclined you may find early news of investment interest and importance in publications like *Datamation* (on computers), *Advertising Age, American Banker,* or *Supermarket News.*

Among general business magazines, the two that most commonly draw attention on Wall Street are *Barron's* and *Forbes. Barron's* is read each weekend by many active participants in the markets for both its broad array of statistical information and its commentary—quite often controversial—on the economy, the markets, and individual industries and companies. One investor told recently of reading a *Barron's* item that contended there was no basis for the high price of a certain speculative stock. The following Monday, he figured, the stock was bound to take a nosedive. When it didn't, he reasoned that investors must have a strong faith indeed in the stock's prospects, and he bought some shares for himself. The stock subsequently doubled before a new *Barron's* item appeared, expressing bafflement at its behavior.

Forbes, while it devotes less attention to short-term market statistics, is also aimed at an audience of active investors. It strikes many readers as opinionated, sometimes even caustic. But its many articles and columns contain a wealth of investment ideas and strategies. Once, when an investor was accused of having traded illegally on inside information, he steadfastly maintained his innocence. He had got, he said, the idea of investing in the company in question from an article in *Forbes.*

Of all the leading business publications, *Fortune* is probably the classiest. It often seems to discuss business as a way of life, even as an art form. Its staff includes some of the best business writers and reporters in this country. It devotes a great deal of attention to matters of concern to investors, while also taking on broad topics of government policy and management. Though its articles on subjects such as America's "toughest bosses" or the progress of a given class of Harvard Business School graduates may be only of indirect interest to people in the course of making their investment decisions, *Fortune* is on the regular reading list of many Wall Street professionals and individual investors.

Business Week has a long-standing reputation as a source of "nuts and bolts" information about individual companies, industries, and economic trends. Of late it has dramatically expanded the space it gives to the securities markets and specific investment developments and ideas. It covers some glamorous industries, such as high technology, and some decidedly unglamorous ones (a potential source of undiscovered investment opportunities), in great depth.

There are other business publications that are far too numerous to discuss, or even to mention, here. Some, like *Money* and *Fact*, are aimed specifically at the individual investor. General-interest magazines of many descriptions now devote much more space than they used to to matters of finance and personal investing. One of the newest phenomena in the publishing world is the regional or local business newspaper or magazine. It's a daunting assignment to try to read all of what is available, though a good many people try. Your selection of regular reading must of necessity depend on your own personal tastes and circumstances.

INVESTMENT ADVISORY SERVICES

You cannot venture very far into the investment jungle without encountering several species of the breed known as independent investment advisers. Some are large firms that can provide you with a great amount of information, as well as opinions and recommendations, on the merits of many investment possibilities. Others are one- or two-person operations that may provide standard "market letter" analyses of the outlook for stocks, or specialize in some specific investment field such as precious metals or convertible securities. Today there are investment advisory services that report on mutual funds, money-market funds, even bank deposit interest rates.

Keeping up with more than a few of these services can be a significant drain on your time as well as your pocketbook. True, the cost of subscribing is tax deductible if you are an active investor. But most services don't come cheap. Among the dozens that have large followings, it may serve you best to look for one or two that seem most harmonious with your investment goals and your view of the world. It is possible to overdose on investment advice; if you are a long-term investor who buys and sells only infrequently, do you really stand to benefit from a "hot line" telephone service that comes out with new recommendations every week or so?

Among the biggest and best-known advisory firms are Value Line Inc., Standard & Poor's Corp., and Moody's Investors Service. Value Line's offerings include quarterly reports on more than 1,600 stocks that pack a great deal of information onto a single page. These are a central part of the Value Line Investment Survey. S&P's *Stock Guide,* revised monthly, is a standard reference tool in the investing world, which your broker may provide at no charge if you are a valued customer. Moody's publishes a quarterly *Handbook of Common Stocks.*

BROKERS AND
SALESPEOPLE

In their quest for investment information, many people turn to brokers and agents who sell products ranging from stocks and bonds to mutual funds, life insurance, and real estate. In any of these fields, there are many knowledgeable, conscientious people who can alert you to possibilities you weren't aware of and answer almost any question you might care to ask. However, you should always be aware that these people have a vested interest in selling you something, or persuading you to sell something you own to somebody else. They are generally paid commissions for each transaction their customers conduct. Try putting yourself in a broker's position for a moment. If you had a lot of hungry mouths to feed (and if some of those mouths were simultaneously incurring heavy orthodontists' bills), would you be inclined to tell a high-rolling customer, "Slow down—you're trading too much for your own good," or, "If I were you, I wouldn't change a thing in your portfolio. All the holdings look good, and they should do well if you just sit tight"?

Seeing a gap in the traditional relationship between broker and customer, many people lately have hung out shingles as "financial planners," implicitly or explicitly promising impartial advice and assistance on matters of investment planning and personal finance. "The legitimate financial planning industry is growing today at an explosive pace," said a 1985 report by the Council of Better Business Bureaus and the North American Securities Administrators Association. "And so is the volume of multi-million-dollar fraud committed by the con men and swindlers who constitute the 'dark side' of this relatively new and unregulated financial service sector."

The report pointed out that there are three types of financial planners, classified by the way in which they make their money: those that simply charge a fee for their services, those that receive commissions for products they sell, and those that collect a combination of fees and commissions. A "fee-only" arrangement might seem to offer the best hope of objective advice, but it is no assurance that you will get your money's worth.

The two associations say that any type of financial planner should provide you with:

- A detailed and understandable financial plan tailored to your specific circumstances
- A discussion of the degree and types of risk you are willing to take in pursuit of your goals
- Specific suggestions for improving your personal cash management
- A full explanation of the assumptions on which your financial plan is based
- A range of alternative investment choices, with a discussion of the potential benefits and hazards of each

- Access to additional advice from other professionals, including lawyers and accountants
- A timetable for monitoring the progress of your financial plan after you have embarked on it.

It seems self-evident that financial planners by the thousands wouldn't be going into business if there weren't a great demand for their services. But however trendy it might be, having your own financial planner might be an unnecessary luxury if you are capable of making your own decisions and satisfied with the results you are achieving. If you are following a relatively simple strategy, it is easy to start worrying: Am I missing out because I'm not deep into tax-sheltered limited partnerships, trusts holding zero-coupon bonds, and so forth? Maybe, but also maybe not. Ignorance can be costly in managing your money. But simplicity can also be a virtue, especially if it comes in the form of a self-devised investment plan with which your instincts are comfortable.

"HOT TIPS"

Unless this is the first investment book you have ever read, you are probably already familiar with the precept "Don't listen to hot tips." No bit of investment advice is so often given, or so often ignored. When a hot tip comes to you from a source you consider reliable, and it is accompanied by a story that seems to back it up, it may be very hard to resist acting on it. How will you feel if you do nothing, and it proves to be correct? "No guts, no glory," whispers the taunting voice in your head.

It is true, many investment advisers agree, that you must take some chances if you want to shoot for big investment rewards. But that does not validate a strategy of rolling the dice every time you hear a hot tip. For one thing, are you really in a position to be privy to reliable, valuable investment information? Is your source really more knowledgeable than all, or most, of the big-time players in the securities markets? If the answer to both those questions is "yes," you still may be courting trouble acting on a hot tip. You could be flirting with the rules that prohibit trading on "inside information."

Beyond that, many students of investing say, there is a fundamental problem with hot tips. They do not fit into any systematic, disciplined approach to investing. How can you pursue any serious long-term goal by running off in random directions at unpredictable intervals whenever a hot tip happens to reach you?

Henry Gailliot, head of an investment policy team at Federated Research Corp., a Pittsburgh-based firm that manages billions in stock and bond portfolios, says a disciplined system is necessary to help an investor overcome the natural human tendencies that cause so many financial mistakes.

Human nature tempts people to buy stocks when the economy looks healthy and the markets are buzzing with optimism. The trouble is, these conditions usually prevail when prices are at a peak, and wise investors are selling, not buying. The best time to buy stocks is often during recessions, when prices are depressed and gloom abounds. But on such occasions, both your head and your heart are likely to be screaming at you to get out of the market and stay out.

Human nature also seems to dictate that the typical investor quickly sells profitable stocks, while holding on to losers in the hope that they sooner or later will come back. This flies in the face of the accepted principle that you are far better off cutting your losses by taking them early, and letting your winners run.

So how do you overcome these self-defeating impulses? Gailliot doesn't suggest that there is an easy, all-encompassing answer, but he says it helps to have a system of discipline that you stick with at all times. His own system involves regular computer screens of 1,000 stocks—something that may be beyond your practical reach. Nevertheless, he says the kind of system you use isn't so important as the fact that you have one and stay with it.

When you set out to buy a stock, he suggests, you should have a clear reason why you think it represents a good value, so clear that you can write it down. Then, he suggests, you might reexamine the investment every six months. If the reason you bought in the first place is no longer valid, he recommends selling the stock, no matter what its price performance has been. "Don't rationalize, looking for some other reason why you should hold onto it," he says.

By the same token, if the reasoning still appears sound, he argues that the stock should be held, even if it seems to be sitting dead in the stock-market waters. Sooner or later, he believes, hidden values in stocks are very likely to be discovered by investors generally, but it is just about impossible to predict when that "sooner or later" will be.

Why don't more investors adopt and stick with a system? Gailliot says it takes persistence, and sometimes courage as well. There are times, he says, when any system, no matter how beautifully conceived, won't seem to be working. Investment fads or extremes of emotion in the marketplace may distort prices far out of proportion to any logic on which your system is based. Furthermore, in putting limits on hunches, sudden impulses, and hot tips, an orderly system takes a lot of the fun out of "playing the market." As Gailliot says, "Discipline is dull."

In seeking to impose some order on your investment strategies, many experts advise, it is helpful to try to examine your motives in buying stocks. Simple, you might say, I want to make money. But it doesn't take a psychologist to point out that the market's appeal to many people goes far beyond questions of dollars and cents. If talk of total return and increased net worth bores you—if you want action, adventure, and a feeling of being savvy, sophisticated and in the know—well, that's what hot tips are for.

RECORD-KEEPING

For tax reasons alone, good record-keeping is a must in the quest for investment success. But well-maintained records can do much more for you than help you keep your accounts square with Uncle Sam. A periodic study of your past and present results can show your strengths and weaknesses as an investor. The plain, unadorned numbers may also serve to dispel any number of misconceptions or delusions you may have about your prowess, or lack thereof, as an investor.

No one specific record-keeping system will suit every investor's needs. Indeed, the best system for you is most likely one you design yourself, tailored to your own tastes. But whether it is kept on file cards or in a personal computer, every system should contain several essential elements.

First of all, it should show you clearly and readily the purchase price, and date of purchase, of any securities you own. Secondly, it should provide you with handy access to your net gains or losses realized for tax purposes in the current tax year. This information is often vital in planning your strategies to maximum after-tax advantage. Most of all, it should help you to stay organized in your investment activities, and allow you to take periodic readings that measure whether you are making satisfactory progress toward your investment goals.

PART

III

THE LANGUAGE OF THE STOCK MARKET

In the course of keeping informed about the investment markets, you naturally are going to read and hear a lot of talk about them. In these money-conscious times (and what times aren't?), investments and the stock market are favorite topics of conversation at social and business gatherings, or almost anywhere else the opportunity arises—whether the scene is a taxicab, a tavern, or a tea party. You may well spend a good deal of time talking on the telephone with your broker or poring over investment advisory letters.

As you do this, you quickly learn that the language of Wall Street often seems to bear little resemblance to the English you learned in school. Perhaps a neighbor confides, "I'm bullish, but my broker says the technical indicators are negative near-term, so I'm waiting for a correction to buy on weakness."

Or you might read something like this actual commentary chosen at random from a popular market letter: "The late-January to early-March decline in the long and short term debt markets clearly violated the bullish trend that had been in effect since last year's May-June lows. While the decline did damage price patterns in the long and short term sectors, it also produced the most positive set of oversold and sentiment conditions since last June. In addition the price stabilization during the first three weeks of March produced definite bottom patterns from which a rally could unfold."

If you're inclined at first to dismiss this kind of thing as gibberish, you're by no means alone. When people talk in Wall Streetese, cynics like to observe, the more impenetrable the verbiage, the more likely it is that the speaker is actually saying, "I haven't the faintest idea what's going to happen."

But of course any group with common interests tends to develop its own specialized way of talking. Truckers who helped create the CB radio craze of the 1970s spoke of a concealed patrol car as "Smokey in the weeds," or referred to an empty trailer they were hauling as "a load of postholes." In decades past, any lunch-counter worker knew that a tuna fish sandwich on toasted rye bread was a "tuna whiskey down."

As almost anyone in the investment world would insist, the language of Wall Street is more than jargon for jargon's sake. The vocabulary of the markets has evolved as a means of trying to make sense of a very complicated environment that defies easy analysis.

As in any other endeavor, some high-flown talk about investments is obfuscation employed, wittingly or unwittingly, by someone trying to make a superficial point sound profound. Some of it is what lawyers call "dealers' talk"—patter aimed at persuading you to buy merchandise. Still, people who have something of real value to say may talk in Wall Street terms too. The trick, not always easily accomplished, is to discern what makes sense and what doesn't. The lexicon that follows is intended to help you in that task.

ARBITRAGE. Suppose there is a rare drought in Seattle, and a succession of rainstorms in normally dry Los Angeles. Umbrellas pile up in warehouses all over the state of Washington, but are almost impossible to find in southern California. Seeing and seizing an opportunity, you contract to buy a large quantity of umbrellas from a Seattle distributor for $1 apiece, simultaneously selling them to a dealer in Los Angeles for $5 each. Your maneuver earns you a healthy profit without requiring you to take any significant risk.

In transacting this deal, you have performed a crude form of arbitrage. In the financial world, a large corps of professional traders monitors the markets worldwide minute by minute, looking for disparities in similar or related commodites or securities. Is gold trading at $X in Zurich and $X plus 5 cents in Tokyo? Then buy lots of it in Zurich, simultaneously sell the same amount in Tokyo, and pocket the difference.

Arbitrageurs, or "arbs," usually are armed with sophisticated sources of information, computers to monitor market fluctuations around the world, communications equipment that allows them to act instantly, and large quantities of capital to invest. There isn't much chance for a small investor to play their game.

However, since they operate in the same markets into which you must venture if you want to buy and sell something like stocks or gold, you are well advised to be aware of their presence. If you come upon a situation that looks like a golden opportunity to cash in on some "underpriced" investment, it might pay to ask yourself why the professionals haven't spotted it already.

Arbitrageurs have been important participants in the wave of corporate takeover activity in the past several years. Suppose Company A offered to acquire Company B by exchanging one of its shares for every two shares of Company B. If A was trading at $21 a share, and B at $10, it made sense to buy a block of B's stock and simultaneously sell an equivalent amount of A's stock short, since A was trading above the two-for-one ratio established by the merger proposal.

There were risks in this strategy: The terms of the deal might be changed, or it might never take place. But it proved profitable enough to encourage arbs to become even more venturesome. Rather than hedging, a trader might simply buy up a large chunk of B's stock, hoping that another bidder would materialize, offering a higher price. Eventually, as their experience and financial strength increased, some professional traders began initiating takeover efforts on their own. At this point they metamorphosed in the press from "arbitrageurs" into "financiers" or "corporate raiders," depending on who was describing them.

BARGAIN-HUNTING. When stock prices turn upward after a period of decline, and there appears to be no ready explanation for this reversal of direction, market commentators often attribute it to "bargain-hunting." The presumption is that stock prices have fallen from levels where people found them unattractive to a point where they looked relatively cheap. When a given security or market has experienced a particularly sharp drop, bargain-hunters are said to be "bottom-fishing."

Of course, all buyers of stocks are looking for bargains, whether the market has been falling for months or has just reached a record high. The metaphor "bottom-fishing" conjures up some vivid negative images, suggesting that you have dropped your hook to depths into which you cannot see, and may snare any manner of detritus that has settled in the mud at the bottom of the lake.

BAROMETERS AND INDICATORS. Meteorologists, professional and amateur, long have known that an increase or decrease in barometric pressure can be a strong signal of an impending change in the weather. Ever since stock trading became a serious endeavor, analysts and participants in the market have been searching for similar ways to anticipate changes in investment trends. Some of the popular investment barometers that have evolved over the years are taken very seriously by their followers; others are whimsical diversions explainable only by historical coincidence. None offers an absolute solution to the riddle posed by the stock market, but some of them—especially those whose premises make the most logical sense—bear watching.

Many Wall Street analysts concentrate on indicators that attempt to measure prevailing sentiment in the marketplace, and to detect extremes of pessimism and optimism (see the discussion of Contrary Opinion that appears later in this section). An example of this type of indicator is the weekly tabulation by Investors Intelligence Inc. of investment advisory services that are bullish, bearish, or predicting a "correction"—an interim decline in stock prices within a long-term rising trend. The theory behind this is that most advisory services are "trend-followers," and therefore tend to be most bullish at market tops—which of course represent the ideal time to be selling stocks—and most bearish at market bottoms, when the wise investor should be working up the nerve to buy. Some skeptics express reservations about relying too much on the Investors Intelligence ratings because, in their view, many advisory services hedge their forecasts to the point that it is hard to classify them in any of the three categories.

Indicators have also been developed that monitor trading in options—*calls* that give their owners the right to buy stocks at specified prices within set periods of time, and *puts* that give their owners the right to sell stocks under the same circumstances. If activity is especially heavy in calls, and prices for these options rise to especially high levels, sentiment is theoretically too bullish, setting the stage for a market decline. Conversely, if puts are all the rage, pessimism is thought to have reached unwarranted extremes.

In their search for clues to the outlook for stocks, some analysts monitor reports of buying and selling by insiders—top executives, directors, and large shareholders. The idea is that, even with all the information public companies must disclose, insiders have a better knowledge of and feeling for how things are going at their companies than outsiders are likely to gain. Experience generally suggests that insiders in the aggregate are indeed a savvy bunch, but that they tend to be early in their actions, buying some months before an upturn in their companies' stocks or selling well in advance of a market top. One problem in the use of insider sales as an investment indicator: Sometimes insiders can be too close to their businesses to see their prospects clearly. At many companies where management owns large amounts of stock and options to buy shares, the price of the stock is a highly emotional subject.

Some indicators have been devised using past calendar patterns of stock-market behavior. Perhaps the best known of these is the January barometer, credited mainly to investment adviser

Yale Hirsch. It holds that, "as January goes, so goes the rest of the year" in the stock market. Advocates of this theory point to figures that show its high percentage of accuracy over the past two or three decades. Its detractors cite instances like 1982, when the market fell in January but then staged a spectacular rally, starting in August, that produced a strong net gain for the year as a whole. They write off whatever past record the indicator might have amassed as a coincidence.

Coincidence most certainly is the progenitor of the famous but foolish Super Bowl indicator. Almost every year since the pro football championship extravaganza began in 1967, the market has risen when a team from the original National Football League has won. Victories by teams with roots in the old American Football League have come at the start of bear market years.

If the outcome of a football game can foreshadow events in the stock market, why not the World Series, or the Kentucky Derby, or the Indianapolis 500? The answer, of course, is that as long as you have enough random possibilities, you are likely to get two statistical series that seem to fit together. Even the main proponents of the Super Bowl indicator readily acknowledge that they publish information on it as an entertaining diversion, not a serious proposition. They said they were astonished when some investors began to take it as a real basis for making financial decisions.

BASIS POINTS. A basis point is .01%—one one-hundredth of a percentage point. If one security yields 9.25 percent and another 8.86 percent, the first has a yield advantage on the other of 39 basis points. Just a few basis points can make a big difference to professional investors who trade interest-bearing securities, frequently in very large amounts. If you could pocket one basis point's worth of the interest paid on $500 million in Treasury bonds for one year, you'd be $50,000 richer.

Few readers of this book are likely to have that opportunity. But many people are faced with basis-point calculations in the course of managing their money. Suppose you must choose between an insured money market deposit account that yields 8.1 percent, and a money fund, highly safe but uninsured, that offers a current return of 8.4 percent. Many people who are eager to maximize the income from their savings might quickly opt for the money fund—and who's to fault them?

Still, it may be helpful to bear in mind that, when dealing with relatively small amounts of money, a few basis points don't amount to much difference over any but very long periods of time. Even a full percentage point (100 basis points) difference in yield on a $5,000 investment is only $50 a year, before any taxes owed are taken into account. If there is a significant difference in safety between the two choices, forgoing the extra $50 might well be a worthwhile purchase of peace of mind.

BLUE CHIPS. Wall street abhors anything that associates its activities with the world of gambling. Nevertheless, the term blue chip appears to have evolved from the fact that, among the betting chips used in games like poker, the blue normally have the highest value (followed by red and white).

On Wall Street, a blue chip is the stock of a company with a long and successful history, usually a prominent position in a healthy industry, and a top credit rating. The definition must of necessity be somewhat vague, since "blue chip" is a relative term. To one observer, it might signify a stock that qualifies for inclusion in the Dow Jones industrial average. To another, it might mean any of the companies that make *Fortune's* annual list of the nation's 500 largest industrial companies.

If it is somewhat hazy, blue chip quality can also be fleeting. Time has taken its toll, for example, on some of the railroad and steel concerns that once ranked at the pinnacle of American business. Furthermore, "stable" and "blue chip" are no longer always synonymous in today's investment world.

In the past couple of decades, large investing institutions have come to play an increasingly dominant role in stock trading. Because of their size, they tend to invest heavily in blue chips. The price of any stock that is heavily owned by institutions can be subject to sudden swings if, for example, the company involved reports earnings that fall short of projections made by Wall Street analysts.

Another point to consider: The growth of options and futures contracts on stock-market indexes has led to a proliferation of trading strategies involving the options or futures and the large stocks that are primary components of the indexes. The professional traders are practicing a form of arbitrage (see above) that has little to do with any individual company's business circumstances. Their maneuvers can increase the short-term volatility of even the bluest of blue chip stocks.

In sum, the phrase "blue chip" always has, and still does, imply high quality. In today's markets, however, it should not necessarily be taken as an assurance of stability or safety.

BOOK VALUE. Book value is the theoretical worth of a company if it were dismantled, all its assets sold and debts paid off, and the net proceeds distributed to shareholders. It is one tool available to investors when they are assessing the worth of a company or looking for stocks at "bargain" prices, but it must be used carefully. Actual liquidations of healthy, going concerns happen very infrequently. So if you buy a stock because it is selling below book value, you should logically have some reason to believe the market will put a higher price on it some time in the future.

Book value relationships tend to vary widely from industry to industry. If a company is in a business that involves a large investment in fixed assets like real estate of sprawling production facilities, its stock may sell at or below book most of the time. On the other hand, if a company's main asset is the brains of its creative staff or marketing department, the stock price may routinely stand far above book value. In any case, an important consideration in investing in any company is how well management uses its assets to produce growth and profits.

Book value can be misleading in another way. For example, a tract of land owned by a company may have appreciated handsomely in value, but still be carried on its books at an obsolete price. In instances like this, the published book value may substantially understate the company's actual worth.

Depending on overall market conditions, stocks selling for less than book value can be either abundant or scarce. According to a tabulation by Standard & Poor's Corp., more than half of all stocks listed on the New York Stock Exchange sold for less than their book values in June 1982, when the market was depressed. Three years later, as the market was making record highs, just 15 percent were trading below book.

BROKER'S RECOMMENDATIONS. In a simple world, a stockbroker would have only four basic recommendations to make: "Buy" or "Don't Buy" in the case of an investment you were considering for purchase; "Sell" or "Keep" in the case of an investment you were thinking about unloading. Since the real world isn't simple, the terminology of recommendations by brokers and investment advisers can be very complicated.

When a stock is a "strong hold," what does that mean? What sort of an endorsement is "buy on weakness"? Some critics of Wall Street analysts contend that expressions like these are cop-outs, designed to protect the broker or adviser from looking bad no matter what happens subsequently.

Maybe so. In return for the high pay and the prestige that goes with the job, you might reason, the least you might expect from a broker or investment adviser is clear, unequivocal advice. But consider for a moment the position of the analyst who follows a company for a brokerage firm.

If he or she puts out a "sell" recommendation on the company's stock, it might naturally make the management of that company angry. So angry, in fact, that it might retaliate by shutting off lines of communication on which the analyst depends for information. Thus a brokerage firm that turns negative on a company's prospects might send out its message by removing the stock from its recommended list, downgrading it from a "buy" to a "hold," or suggesting a "switch" to another stock.

In the last few years, there has been something of a trend back toward more basic language in evaluating and recommending stocks. Some brokerage firms and the Value Line Investment Survey have numerical codes of, say, 1 to 5, which they use to rank stocks in order of their presumed desirability. Another investment advisory service, Standard & Poor's *The Outlook,* has occasionally published lists of "stocks to avoid."

No matter what the terminology employed, of course, brokers' and advisers' recommendations are only as helpful as the quality of research and judgment behind them. Some investors want a lot of professional advice; others prefer to make decisions on their own.

BULL AND BEAR MARKETS. The bull and the bear go back a long time as basic images of life in the financial world. A bull is someone who expects a rise in prices for a given investment or investments, and thus by extension is an optimist. A bear expects declining prices, and may seek to profit from them by selling short (see Long and Short). Since optimism tends to be good for business on Wall Street, and pessimism not so good for business, the number of outspoken optimists tends to be much greater at any given time than the number of vocal pessimists. As the old saying succinctly puts it, "Nobody loves a bear."

There are several somewhat vague explanations around for the origins of the two terms. One is that a bull attacks its foe with its horns in a rising arc, while a bear strikes downward from above. In any case, both can be powerful, violent creatures, which makes them apt symbols for the markets they represent.

The expression "bull market" is used to describe a period of lasting and significant increases in the prices of most stocks or other securities. A bear market, naturally, is just the opposite—an extended decline. Moves in security prices that prove to be false starts are sometimes called bear or bull traps. Bull and bear markets generally can be identified clearly on charts of the past. Alas, they are not always so easily discerned while they are happening.

The bull and bear symbolism encourages reference to other forms of animal life in discussing investments. Optimists who admit that they are not too confident of their case may describe themselves as "chicken bulls." Then, too, there is the old admonition against being too greedy in quest of investing profits: "Either a bull or a bear can make money, but never a pig."

CAPITALIZATION. Before investing in any stock, it is a good idea to familiarize yourself with its market value—the number of shares outstanding times the price of each share. This figure, often referred to as the stock's capitalization, can tell you some important things about the kind of market it is likely to enjoy, as well as what types of investors are likely to trade in it. Issues with high market values are sometimes called "big-cap" stocks, and those with lower total values "small-cap" or "low-cap" stocks.

Large capitalization is a hallmark of eminence in the investment world. The number of shares alone isn't enough to tell the story. If a new, speculative company somehow manages to float a 20 million-share offering at 5 cents apiece, it is worth only $1 million in the market. Nor is a high price per share by itself a reliable guide. A company that has, say, 500,000 shares in public hands at a price of $50 apiece isn't likely to attract a wide following among investing institutions. There simply isn't enough stock available to justify their taking the trouble to follow the company.

But if both the number of shares and the price of each share are reasonably large, the company is certified by the market to have substantial value. Furthermore, it has a good chance of enjoying an active market—one in which you can expect to find a ready seller when you want to buy, at a price not too far from that of the last trade. This *liquidity* becomes an even more important question when you want to sell. A basic precept of managing money in any investment holds that nothing should be bought without a good idea of how, when, and where you can hope to sell it in the future.

No matter how much they would like to, large institutions cannot exploit small-capitalization stocks to any great degree. They cannot take a substantial position in such stocks without pushing the price up materially. A small position does not do them much good either, since it does not stand to have a perceptible impact on their overall results. The limited potential rewards make it a chancy proposition for them to devote much time and expense to studying small stocks.

The individual investor faces no such constraints. Indeed, it is the dream of many a stock-market aficionado to discover and buy a small-cap stock, and to sell it some time later when it has gone big-cap. With all its allure, this strategy is normally riskier than buying stocks that already enjoy active markets because of their healthy capitalization.

CONTRARY OPINION. Experts on financial matters may disagree about many things. But few quarrel with the basic precept that to be successful in investing, you must stay clear of—and even go against—the conventional wisdom and assumptions made by the crowd. If some fact is widely known or some theory is widely accepted, it is very likely that it is already reflected in the prices of stocks that stand to be affected. The greatest opportunity for investors may lie instead in the possibility that the fact is misunderstood by most people, or that the theory will prove to be wrong.

To turn this approach to investing into a regular discipline, many followers of the stock market seek to apply contrary opinion. In its simplest definition, it may be described as the classic effort to buy low and sell high. Devoted contrarians have constructed systems elaborate enough to fill a book. The ultimate philosophical problem with contrary opinion is that, by definition, it can be practiced successfully only by a minority of investors.

The doctrine of contrary opinion may be readily understood, but that doesn't mean it is easy to put into practice. It may require a bold approach when the prevailing mood is cautious and gloomy, and a willingness to cash in your chips at a time when everybody is talking about how much money there is to be made. As Joseph Feshbach, a technical analyst on Wall Street, put it: "Contrarians are never comfortable at the same time everyone else is."

CORRECTIONS. In Wall Street jargon, a correction occurs when a market rally or bull market is interrupted (but not ended) by an interim period of declining prices. After a rise in the Dow Jones industrial average of, say, 150 points, brokers may begin to talk of the possibility of a 75-point decline that they imply, or even declare, would be beneficial for the market's long-term outlook. At times this word can be an irritating euphemism for a plain old drop in the market, especially to someone who bought just before the decline started. To say that a drop in stock prices somehow corrects things is not a very palatable notion to the person whose net worth is being corrected.

Nevertheless, it makes sense that the market cannot go straight up forever. After a spree of enthusiastic buying, investors at some point exhaust their ammunition—that is, most of them have already turned bullish and poured their available funds into stocks. Prices may have reached the point where anyone left with money to invest considers stocks too expensive and too risky. A correction at this stage is supposed to alleviate those problems and set the stage for a new advance.

For that to happen, it stands to reason that the correction must cut deep enough to lessen optimism, increase fear, and produce a wary buildup of cash reserves among investors. The correction doesn't end until a significant number of market participants come to suspect that it is something more than just a temporary retreat. The word "correction" has been heard in the early stages of many a painful market decline. On those occasions, the people who used it were anything but correct.

CYCLICAL STOCKS. Despite all efforts to get it on a smooth, steady path of growth, the U.S. economy is still prone to cycles—expansion followed by slowdown and quite often recession, then recovery leading to expansion again. Some companies and industries feel the effects of these cycles more than others. And those that are highly sensitive don't always suffer or thrive at the same stage of the process. The housing industry, for example, has historically been among the first to feel the pinch of rising interest rates, as mortgages and financing for builders become more expensive.

When brokers speak of cyclical stocks, they are usually referring to those companies and industries whose health and profitability most closely track the charts of economic data like the gross national product and industrial production. Examples are steel, paper, and chemicals. In modern, high-technology times, machine-tool and semiconductor stocks have also acquired a cyclical reputation. In theory, the best time to buy cyclical stocks is just before the market begins to anticipate a period of rapid economic growth. Any company of this description, of course, must also be evaluated on its specific merits, and in the light of other opportunities and obstacles it faces—for example, notable success in cost-cutting, or persistent problems with foreign competition.

DEFENSIVE STOCKS. By contrast with cyclical stocks, so-called defensive issues are considered to be relatively immune to the ups and downs of the economy. The goods and services produced by companies in this category tend to sell at a relatively steady rate in good times or bad, so their earnings don't boom when the economy soars, but neither do they plunge in recessions. A standard working list of defensive issues would include makers of consumer products like food, soap, cosmetics, and soft drinks, and perhaps selected electric, gas, and telephone utilities.

As this description may attest, defensive stocks tend to rank among the top performers in periods when the market in general is falling, and to lag well behind when the general market is doing well. Of course, a defensive stock that suddenly becomes a takeover target or finds some means of accelerating its earnings growth can be transformed into a high-flyer. And conversely, a company in this league that makes serious miscalculations or is hit by some unexpected calamity can leave its shareholders feeling quite defenseless.

DISCOUNTING EFFECT. When some seemingly important news breaks, but the stock market and the stocks of companies most likely to be affected fail to respond, the market is often said to have discounted the news in advance. This may seem a puzzling phenomenon to the uninitiated, but it makes eminent sense once you stop to think it through. Investors do not wait for news to become official before they respond to it. Indeed, they tend to act as soon as they start to suspect that the development in question might occur in the future.

Consider the case in which the stock of an airline, which is only modestly profitable at present, rises on news of declining prices for crude oil. The oil has not even been refined into jet fuel yet, but investors have immediately reached the conclusion that dropping fuel prices will help improve the carrier's earnings in future quarters by reducing its operating costs. Many other factors, of course, will affect the airline's bottom line. But there has been no very recent change in investors' perception of those other factors, and thus the drop in oil prices has raised the market's appraisal of the company's outlook.

By the time the airline reports improved profits six months or a year later, the news comes as no surprise at all. Some investors who bought at the time that oil prices were falling may actually choose the occasion of the earnings report as an opportune moment to cash in the profits they had been hoping for. So the ''good news'' of higher earnings may be met with a decline in the stock's price. This is rational, not perverse, behavior. It would be perverse for investors not to act in what they see as their own self-interest on future expectations, rather than current events.

Just how good is the stock market at discounting the future?

If the market sees all and knows all, and adjusts immediately to every change in expectations, is there any point in trying to beat it? Those questions lie at the heart of a long-running and heated debate over the efficient-market theory, discussed in a separate entry below.

DOLLAR-COST AVERAGING. How can you consistently buy stocks or other investments at "low" prices, and sell when their prices are "high"? Huge amounts of time and trouble have been devoted to that question over the years. And while many people claim to have found successful methods and systems to achieve good results, it remains a challenging mission that isn't likely to get easier in the future.

The simplest approach is simply not to try to "time" the market at all, but rather to invest regular sums periodically in securities you believe to be appealing for the long term. You won't get the best price possible, unless you are outlandishly lucky, but a phenomenon known as dollar-cost averaging will work in your favor.

The principle that underlies dollar-cost averaging is the fact that when identical amounts of money are invested at differing prices, the money buys more shares at low prices than it does at high prices. Over time, this works in the buyer's favor even in a neutral market. Consider the following example:

You invest $1,000 in the Imaginary Growth Fund when its net asset value stands at 10; another $1,000 six months later when the asset value is at 9; another $1,000 a year later when the asset value stands at 11; and still another $1,000 six months thereafter, when the net asset value is back at 10. You started buying at 10 and, $4,000 later, the fund is still at 10. But your investment is worth more than $4,000—$4,020.20, excluding any dividends and capital gains received and the extra money those payouts might have earned had they been reinvested. The more money invested over time, and the more volatile the price of the security, the greater the effect becomes.

Dollar-cost averaging bears understanding for any long-term investor. It should not, however, be considered the infallible key to wealth-building. For one thing, it cannot work to full advantage without an enduring commitment on the part of the investor. This commitment requires good judgment as well as a great deal of faith. If you follow a dollar-cost averaging strategy in a poor investment that keeps declining in price, you must face the possibility that you are throwing good money after bad.

EFFICIENT-MARKET THEORY. Years ago, people in the academic world began to propose the theory that the stock market was largely efficient—that is, it instantaneously adjusted the prices of stocks to reflect all that was known, expected, or suspected that could affect individual stocks or the market. In simplest terms, their hypothesis was that it was futile to try to ''beat'' the market, since only unknown (and unknowable) future events would cause prices to rise or fall. Some managers of money achieved superior performance, of course, but their results were primarily the result of random selection and could not be expected to continue in the future unless luck stayed with them. Wall Street's professional analysts and money managers hotly dispute this idea, not only because most of them believe they are good at what they do, but also because it implies that their work is unnecessary and unproductive, if not worthless.

In this discussion, there is no intention of delving into the intricacies of this argument or all its philosophical implications. It is something for every investor to be aware of, however. From the 15-Minute Investor's working point of view, it is probably safe to operate on these assumptions:

• The stock market, and other markets, are ''efficient'' at least to some extent. When a big company is owned by hundreds of institutions and followed by dozens of analysts, its stock is most likely to be highly efficient. When you happen on an obscure company and have some special knowledge of its future promise, you may have discovered a pocket of ''inefficiency.''

• The more people come to believe that the market is efficient, and stop trying to beat it, the less efficient it may become. Efficiency, to a great extent, is the result of research and analysis done by people trying to spot "inefficiencies."

• If the market is totally efficient, then all the takeover artists of the modern era who buy stocks and companies in the belief that those securities are selling for less than they are worth must be misguided in their efforts. Since these investors are often willing to pay a good deal more than the market price for stocks of many companies, some commentators have argued, the market itself must be something less than perfectly efficient as a mechanism for putting a fair value on corporations.

EMERGING GROWTH STOCKS. Many analysts, money managers and individual investors make a specialty of following these companies and their stocks, which are also sometimes referred to as "junior growth stocks." There is no mystery why: The impulse is strong among many investors to find companies that have strong growth prospects while still in the early stages of development. The problem in doing this, which is also readily apparent, lies in the fact that youthful companies face many potential pitfalls before they can reach prosperous maturity.

As it emerges from the early stages of its development, a company's bright energetic managers typically must learn to think and operate in new ways. A genius who can bring a new product or service from a mere vision to reality may have a great deal of trouble managing an enterprise once he or she must delegate more and more of its operations to others. In addition, success in many cases breeds competition.

For conservative, long-term investors, many advisers recommend using a package approach to emerging growth stocks—assembling a portfolio of, say, a half dozen investments of this type and waiting patiently for them to develop. Many an emerging-growth success story has been punctuated by chapters in which it appears the whole business is going to unravel. With a diversified approach, furthermore, only one or two stocks need to fulfill their promise to offset losses from other holdings that don't work out. Individual investors who don't want to do their own research can select from a variety of mutual funds whose specific strategy is focused on emerging growth issues.

At any given time, investors as a group seem to view emerging growth stocks either with great enthusiasm or with utter disdain. For that reason, emerging-growth portfolios, either self-assembled or in a mutual fund, tend to be very volatile over the short run. Also, the 15-Minute Investor should be aware that there is no standard that must be met for a stock to be touted as an emerging growth issue. The label can be, and has been, applied to new and small stocks whose investment merits may be very dubious.

EXECUTION. This term refers to the adroitness, or lack of it, with which a brokerage firm fulfills your orders to buy and sell securities in the marketplace. Particularly in turbulent markets, good execution—speedy, skillful service—can make a substantial difference in the price you pay or receive. When you are deciding whether to use a "full-service" or discount broker, a registered representative at a full-service firm may argue that its traders can execute orders more skillfully than the discounter's, and thus that the full commission it charges you may actually be a bargain. No evidence has been presented to date that a given full-service broker can be expected to provide consistently better execution than a quality discounter can.

Since execution is at least partly an art, it is difficult for an individual investor to measure. Active traders may develop a feel for which firms provide them with what they consider to be top-flight service. Investors who buy and sell infrequently may have to rely mostly on a firm's reputation. If you feel an order of yours has been executed so poorly that you have been done an injustice, you are perfectly within your rights to complain, to consider taking your future business elsewhere, or both.

FUNDAMENTAL ANALYSIS. The standard, time-honored approach to seeking investment profits is fundamental analysis of the factors that would seem to make a given security or market attractive or unattractive. In the case of the stock market as a whole, a fundamental analyst might consider present and projected future trends in the economy, interest rates, political trends, the apparent intentions of the Federal Reserve, the changing trends and tastes in American society and the world marketplace, and quite possibly many other factors.

To bring fundamental analysis to a single stock or industry group, the analyst would superimpose on all of the above a study of the company's or industry's financial condition and prospects, its competitive position in the economy, the "quality" of its top managers, and so on. Fundamental analysts who follow a company like Hypothetical Industries might give close study to its periodic financial reports and other public disclosures, and talk to Hypothetical's competitors, suppliers and, where possible, its customers.

The task facing the fundamental analyst—and a formidable one it can be—is to uncover information and reach conclusions that are already not generally known to the investing public. Some fundamental analysts, overtly or more subtly, incorporate some elements of technical analysis (see separate entry) into their work. A "pure" fundamentalist may look upon technical analysis with great distaste.

GLAMOUR STOCKS. In the 1960s and early 1970s, professional money managers seeking strong and dependable earnings growth created a sort of elite group of stocks that came to be known as glamour issues, or the "favorite 50" or sometimes the "nifty 50." They were also described as "one-decision" stocks that could be bought and presumably held indefinitely, since there was no end in sight to their growth prospects.

With the advantage of hindsight, it is easy to see many flaws in this line of thinking. It was a fad, and all fads in the investment world sooner or later give way to disillusionment. So many money managers loaded up on these stocks that their prices reached exaggerated levels, reflecting impossibly high expectations. The old adage that "no tree grows to the sky" evidently was totally forgotten.

Some of the glamour issues, such as International Business Machines, are top names in the investment world to this day. Nearly all of the companies involved were unquestioned success stories, at least at the time of their greatest vogue. But the bear market of 1973–74 was exceptionally unkind to many investors who bought these stocks at their peak. Polaroid shares, for example, fell from just under 150 in 1972 to about 25 in 1974; Avon Products from about 140 to 25. As the stock market rebounded in the mid-1970s, many investors remained wary of glamour stocks for a long time. Today, quite possibly because of the bad memories it evokes, the term is seldom used on Wall Street.

GROUP ROTATION. People on Wall Street are fond of pointing out that "it's a market of stocks, not a stock market." What they mean by this is clear to anyone who has ever seen the market "soar" on a day when his or her pet stock drops ⅝ of a point. Even on an outstanding day for the market, perhaps one-third of all issues traded will be unchanged or show a minus figure in the net change column of the stock tables. This phenomenon is attributable in part to the fact that individual stocks often are affected by developments that have no bearing on the market as a whole. It also occurs because the popularity of any given sector of the market may increase or decrease even while the market as a whole is steadily advancing.

The shift of interest from one sector of stocks to another is often called group rotation on Wall Street. Active traders and professional money managers may seek to sense this kind of movement early on, and to switch out of yesterday's hot group into tomorrow's. For most individual investors, this endeavor is difficult and costly—both in time and in brokerage commissions. A patient investor operating from a long-term perspective may choose instead to ignore short-term changes in market vogues. In fact, such an investor may opt to buy stocks of his or her liking in periods when they are neglected by the market, hoping to profit when those stocks once again move into the spotlight.

INTEREST-SENSITIVE STOCKS. More often than not in recent years, the stock market as a whole has been strongly influenced by the ups and downs of interest rates. One reason is that stocks, as a class of investments, compete with bonds for investors' favor. As interest rates rise, they increase the yields available to new buyers of bonds. When rates fall, bonds become less attractive to new investment money coming into the securities marketplace.

In addition, movements in interest rates cause ripple effects in the economy that can lead to business slowdowns or recoveries that are of primary concern to stock-market investors. In theory at least, rising interest rates discourage activity that involves the use of credit—for example, home-building and buying—as well as investment in new business projects of many kinds. Falling rates tend to stimulate these activities. As in most economic matters, cause-and-effect relationships like these are rarely so simple. Still, professional investors in the 1980s often react instinctively to declining interest rates as bullish for the stock market, and to rising rates as bearish for stocks.

Beyond all this, some individual stocks and industry groups are perceived as more closely linked to interest rates than others. The growth and earnings of a service company with little or no debt may progress undisturbed by any but the most severe fluctuations in rates. By contrast, a company that borrows large amounts of money in the routine course of its business may depend heavily on favorable interest-rate conditions to produce successful operating results. As they accustomed themselves to a new era of volatile interest rates over the past decade, Wall Street analysts came to identify certain stocks as interest-sensitive.

A prime example of this kind of issue is a savings and loan holding company. Suppose, for example, that a given savings and loan has issued a large number of long-term mortgages at an average interest rate of 9.5 percent. The S&L can make a tidy profit on the interest from these loans if its own cost of borrowing (the current prevailing level of interest rates) is, say, 7.5 percent. When money costs 9.5 percent, the mortgages are no longer profitable, and indeed there is nothing left to cover the S&L's operating costs, such as salaries. At 11.5 percent, the institution is, in the vernacular, "under water." But if investors believe that rates are about to fall from that 11.5 percent level back into single digits, they may scramble to buy the company's stock anyway, in anticipation of improved operating results in the future.

Utilities—electric, gas, and telephone companies—are another group commonly typed as interest-sensitive. These companies are heavy users of borrowed money to finance their capital expenditures. Futhermore, their stockholders tend to be very yield-conscious, and therefore especially susceptible to the alternative charms of interest-bearing investments like bonds.

The awareness that a given company and its stock are interest-sensitive in no way precludes the need for investigation of its individual circumstances before you invest. A utility that is experiencing worsening problems with a nuclear-power project, for example, may derive scant benefit from a decline in interest rates. An investor who wants to speculate on future changes in interest rates may find purer "plays" in the options and futures markets, if he or she has the means and temperament to venture into these specialized arenas.

INVESTING INSTITUTIONS. Perhaps the simplest definition of an investing institution is an organization that buys, holds, and sells securities with money that has been entrusted to it by others. Institutions like banks have played an active role in the American securities markets since the nation's earliest years. In the past few decades, however, institutions have come to dominate activity in those markets as never before. In the 1950s and 1960s, the mutual fund industry blossomed, and insurance companies, college endowment funds, and other financial organizations began putting more and more money into securities such as stocks.

Without doubt the single most important force in the rise of the institutions has been the dramatic growth of private and public pension plans in this country. Today, institutionalized investment for retirement plans has become a major industry. There are officers at corporations, governmental entities, unions, and professional groups whose job it is to oversee pension funds for their employees or members. These officers may manage money "in-house," making their own investment decisions; they may hire outside management firms to do the work for them; or they may do a combination of both.

By now the role of the institutions in the stock market has become legendary. When the Securities Industry Association, a Wall Street trade group, began a study of trading activity in May–June 1985, it found that institutions accounted for about 62 percent of all "public" trading volume on the New York Stock Exchange. When activity by exchange members for their own accounts was included in the calculations, the institutions' share was still nearly half of the total.

Any group with such clout is bound to attract critics. The modern institutions have often been portrayed as clumsy elephants prone to stampeding in and out of stocks at a moment's emotional provocation. In doing so, they make a big mess in the marketplace without gaining much benefit for themselves or their clients. They are handsomely compensated for their supposed prudence, wisdom, and expertise—yet when the performance figures come in, the results they achieve are often inconsistent or consistently mediocre.

All that may be true. Yet some observant commentators point out that the main fault probably lies in the system itself rather than the people who operate within it. Pension managers in particular are hired to perform a long-term mission; then their bosses and clients hire and fire them based on results achieved in a single year or quarter. When you consider the fact that institutions, to a great degree, *are* the market, it is illogical to expect that a large percentage of them can regularly *beat* the market.

Of what relevance is this to the 15-Minute Investor? Well, first of all, when the "little" individual ventures into the investment jungle, it makes sense to know something about the behavior of the elephants, and to keep an eye on them. You might employ a strategy of staying out of their way by concentrating on small stocks in which they have little interest. Or you might try to get an exciting, and profitable, ride on their backs by seeking out stocks they are just beginning to discover for themselves.

LEADERSHIP. When the stock market is rising, many Wall Street analysts look for those issues that seem to be leading the way—the stocks, or groups of stocks, that are showing the most strength and attracting the most attention. If enthusiasm is high for a broad range of quality stocks, the market may be described as enjoying good leadership. If the liveliest action is in an untested or speculative group of companies, it may be interpreted as a poor portent for the market outlook.

After casino gambling was legalized in Atlantic City, New Jersey, in the 1970s, a very hot market developed in gambling stocks—casino operators, makers of slot machines, any company that stood to benefit from what looked like a major new surge of growth in the legal-gambling business. After a while, some Wall Streeters came to take a very chary view of this group of stocks as market leaders.

About the same time, a similar situation arose involving one of the nation's largest and most financially powerful industries—oil. As oil prices skyrocketed, investors naturally were attracted to companies that owned precious energy assets or were engaged in the business of finding new sources of oil. But the thought struck many investors that what was good for the energy business might be bad for many other parts of the economy. For a time, rising prices for oil stocks seemed to act as a depressant on the rest of the stock market—an ultimate example of negative leadership.

A few individual stocks are presumed to occupy natural leadership roles in the stock market because of their preeminence. General Motors was long considered a "bellwether" stock whose individual price action could set the tone for the market as a whole, and perhaps even provide a signal about the future course of stock prices. Today the bellwether label is most commonly assigned to International Business Machines—partly because "Big Blue" symbolizes progress, on a very large scale, through technology and widely admired management, and partly because it is by far the Number One holding of investing institutions.

LONG AND SHORT. These are two of the most familiar words in the vocabulary of Wall Street—and yet sometimes the source of great confusion among nonprofessional participants in, and followers of, the markets. At the most basic level, you have a long position when you own a security and stand to benefit from an increase in its price; you are short when you have sold a security and stand to benefit from a decline in its price. In our economic and social system, taking a long position—buying— is a readily understandable, natural, positive thing to do. If it works out badly, well, better luck next time.

But going short—selling something you don't own? It has no common analogy in the consumer marketplace, and it may strike a newcomer as a shady as well as a risky practice. Furthermore, it is bearish investors who sell short and, as we have said elsewhere, nobody loves a bear. Selling a stock short *is* more complicated then buying one. To do so, you must borrow the shares first (usually from your broker), and you must follow rules, pay costs, and take risks that aren't involved in going long. It may not be a recommended practice for politicians, corporate chief executives, financial reporters, or other people in positions of some degree of public trust. But it is a legal act performed all the time by upstanding citizens.

When you sell a stock short, you must eventually buy it back to return it to the broker or other person from whom you borrowed it. This purchase is known as *covering* your short position. Brief rallies in the stock market are sometimes ascribed to *short-covering* when a clearer explanation is lacking. The number of shares of a given stock or in a given market that have been sold short and not yet bought back collectively make up the *short interest*. In a stock with a very large short interest, traders may buy in hopes of a *short squeeze,* in which the demand for stock to cover short positions drives the price up drastically.

In today's markets, many sophisticated investors—including individuals who have devoted some study to the subject—take simultaneous long and short positions in similar or related securities. Their purpose in this is often to minimize or even to eliminate risk. Offsetting transactions of this type are known as hedges.

MARGIN. When investors use money borrowed from their brokers to finance part of the cost of buying securities, they are said to be buying on margin. To do this, they must have a *margin account* with a brokerage firm. Before you can open a margin account, you must meet certain eligibility standards.

Margin may be used for several purposes. Speculators employ it to gain leverage, the chance to seek enhanced rewards while taking commensurately increased risk. Here is a simplified example: A stock bought at 10 rises to 15. If you paid $1,000 cash for 100 shares at 10, and received $1,500 when you sold at 15, you would realize a 50 percent return on your money. If, instead, you borrowed half the original purchase cost, and paid off the $500 loan when you sold, you would have turned a $500 initial investment into $1,000—for a 100 percent return.

As for the increased risk, suppose a stock bought at 10 falls to 5. The cash buyer suffers a 50 percent loss. The margin buyer loses his or her total investment, after paying off the $500 loan.

If you have a margin account, you may borrow against securities you hold in that account to make other investments or even a consumer purchase such as a car. Interest rates on margin loans are normally quite low compared with rates on standard bank loans or credit cards. However it is used, a margin loan is typically based on marketable securities as collateral. If these securities decline in value, the borrower may receive a *margin call,* a notice from the broker that more cash or securities must be deposited in the account. If a margin call goes unanswered, the broker can and will sell enough securities in the account to bring it back within specified credit limits.

Margin rules vary among the various types of securities. In the futures markets, for example, they are very liberal. By contrast, when you speculate in put and call options, the use of margin is not allowed. When one Wall Streeter was asked to explain the reason for this proscription, she replied: "When you buy a lottery ticket, you pay the full price."

MARKET-MAKER. Some newcomers to the world of the securities markets find the phrase "making a market" a bit puzzling. But the function market-makers serve is basically very simple and essential to providing a system for continuous trading in stocks and several other types of investments. Brokers who act as market-makers on the trading floors of stock exchanges are known as *specialists.* Elsewhere, such as in the over-the-counter stock market, they are referred to as market-makers or *dealers.*

Both specialists and dealers stand ready at any time under normal business circumstances to buy or sell securities to which they have been assigned or in which they have chosen to trade. Their operations are in many ways analogous to those of, say, an antique dealer, who provides a convenient place for people to turn when they wish either to sell or to buy items that are valued for their age, character, beauty, and scarcity. Like an antique dealer, a specialist seeks to make a profit by buying low and selling high, to the extent that competition and the rules of the marketplace permit.

Frequently, in Wall Street research reports discussing or recommending over-the-counter stocks, a footnote will indicate that the firm publishing the report makes a market in the stock in question. This is worth noting, since account executives at the firm may be given incentives to encourage their customers to trade in such stocks. A "makes a market" footnote does not automatically mean that the recommendation is suspect. It does, however, suggest that the broker with whom you are dealing may not be absolutely objective about its merits.

PAR. At the time of their original sale to the public, many securities are assigned a nominal par value. In the case of investments like stocks whose value is set by market conditions, the par value is generally a meaningless figure. In the market for interest-bearing securities, par refers to the face value of a bond. Before it reaches maturity, a bond trades "at par" only when the interest it pays exactly matches the current yield available on competing investments with identical or near-identical characteristics. At maturity, par value becomes the bond's actual cash redemption value, assuming that the issuer is able to live up to its contractual commitment to pay off and retire the debt.

PENNY STOCKS. In general, the term penny stock is used to describe speculative issues that trade for less than $5 a share. More specifically, it denotes an issue brought to the public and traded afterwards by specialized investment firms operating separately from the big-name stock exchanges and the NASDAQ over-the-counter market. Penny stocks bear roughly the same relationship to blue chips that a speedboat does to an ocean liner. Make that a leaky speedboat.

Yale Hirsch, in his investment letter *Ground Floor,* had this to say about these stocks:

Many of the companies that go public in a hot new-issue market have little reality to them—they are sometimes simply vehicles for wresting money from the public.

Don't just act on hot tips: Be sure to get prospectuses and to read them carefully.

Beware of high-pressure "boiler room" sales pitches such as telephone calls to your home at night by brokers you have never heard of. Don't let brokers keep you from selling when you want to. It's easy to buy new penny stocks, but often nearly impossible to sell.

Beware of cavernous spreads between bid and asked prices—they can run as much as 50 percent, even 100 percent, in some penny stocks. And don't count on getting the quoted bid price when you want to take that nifty 500 percent gain. Bid prices sometimes border on fiction.

Look for companies that have real operations—full-time management as opposed to a lawyer who runs the company part-time out of his lower lefthand drawer; stocks with lots of active market-makers and narrow spreads; and brokers you know.

PREMIUMS AND DISCOUNTS. These two words are used so many different ways on Wall Street that they can often leave a neophyte hopelessly confused. Basically, a premium is the amount by which the price of a given security stands *above* its intrinsic value or some other standard; a discount is the amount by which the price may stand *below* that benchmark.

That's easy enough for anyone with experience as a shopper for consumer goods to remember: Premium goods are "expensive," and discount merchandise is "cheap." It is worthwhile, for example, when considering a stock for purchase to determine whether it is selling at a premium to, or a discount from, its book, or liquidating value. It is helpful to check whether its price-earnings ratio stands at a premium to, or a discount from, the "market multiple"—the average PE ratio for all stocks.

Unfortunately, the two terms also may have other meanings. When an option contract is "written," or created, the amount paid by the buyer of the option and received by the seller is called the premium. Treasury bills are sold at a discount from their face value, but the difference constitutes the interest the buyer receives, and it may tell you little about whether a given T-bill is a bargain or not. Then of course there is the Federal Reserve's discount rate, the interest rate it charges on loans to private financial institutions. A dictionary of financial terms published some years ago defined the discount rate as "the rediscount rate." When the reader hunted back through the pages for "rediscount rate," the definition found was "the discount rate."

An experienced investor may have no trouble following the meaning when a broker says, "This stock is trading at a pretty big premium to the market, but I don't think it has discounted all the good news that's coming." If you can't make any sense out of such a statement, sacrifice your pride (and maybe save yourself some hard-earned money)—ask for an English translation.

PROFIT-TAKING. It's hard to think of an expression more fondly and frequently spoken on Wall Street than this one. It serves as a blanket explanation for market declines when there is no readily apparent reason why prices should be falling. Furthermore, it conveys the impression that the game has just temporarily died down because some happy winners have achieved their financial goals.

Profit-taking has long been an irresistible target for financial writers with an eye for obfuscation. Why, they have asked, is there never any talk about loss-taking? Showing perhaps a bit of exasperation, one prominent magazine writer finally declared: "There is no such thing as profit-taking."

He had a point. For quite a while in the Business News department of The Associated Press, there was an informal ban on the term in market stories, along with such other tired patter as "backing and filling," "traders took to the sidelines," and "prices eased" (when the fact was that they declined, probably not to the ease of everyone involved). Then, when the stock market rose to record highs in the past few years, it became inescapably clear that a good many investors must be engaged in something that could be called profit-taking.

Conclusion: When a prolonged, powerful rise in stock prices is followed by a brief decline, profit-taking may be a plausible, if not very illuminating, way to account for the drop. By the same reasoning, attributing a brief rally in a bear market to profit-taking verges on the absurd.

SECONDARY STOCKS. This catch-all phrase refers to the many issues in the market that rank in the middle ground between blue chips and speculative "cats and dogs." Neither big nor small, neither famous nor notorious, these stocks may nevertheless tell the 15-Minute Investor a lot about what is going on in the market. If stocks of well-managed regional banks; medium-sized retailers; and manufacturers of hoses, clips, pipe, and specialty plastics are advancing quietly but steadily to new highs, the inference might well be drawn that the market is benefiting from broad-based enthusiasm among investors. Many Wall Street analysts like to see secondary stocks do well, but not too well. A frenzied rush to buy shares of companies not yet big enough or strong enough to qualify for blue-chip status may be a sign that the market is starting to suffer from an imbalance of greed over fear.

SPECIAL SITUATIONS. Like snowflakes, no two stocks are exactly alike—even when they all seem to be falling at the same time. Some, however, are more different than others. At times, a given company may offer the promise of uncommon rewards because it is going through a fundamental change. Perhaps new management has taken the necessary steps to turn a chronic money-losing enterprise into a healthy, profitable one. Or maybe the controlling family of a closely held company is considering selling out as its founder-chairman grows old. A new product, a budding new market for an old product, or possibly the divestiture of an old product line that has been a drag on operating results in recent years—all these may represent what Wall Street calls special situations.

The incentive to search out such opportunities in the stock market is readily apparent. In a very real sense, every venturesome investor in stocks looks for special situations. Who wants an ordinary one? That, among other things, makes the task of seeking out and capitalizing on special-situation stocks a challenging and chancy proposition. Many sophisticated professionals devote all their working hours to it. In fact, if you would prefer to hire one of them to play the game for you instead of making the effort yourself, you can choose from a variety of special-situation mutual funds.

Special-situation stocks typically come with a "story," a romantic tale that serves as a ready-made sales pitch for brokers to use. When you hear such a story—whether it is told by your broker, your barber, or your brother-in-law—it makes sense to ask some unromantic questions. Does it ring true from a business standpoint? How many ways could it go awry, and what are the odds that any of those misfortunes could occur? Lastly, and often most importantly, how many other people have heard the story already?

SPREADS. Of the many ways financial institutions make money to cover their costs and earn a profit, spreads are among the most important. A bank, for example, offers to borrow from you (accept deposits) at 8 percent interest, and to lend money to you at 13.5 percent interest. Emotionally, you may regard this financial fact of life as an outrage. But intellectually, you might well conclude that this is only a common, everyday, capitalistic practice. Without the hope of profit, who would bother to establish and operate a bank? Supermarkets, department stores, and car dealers all sell their goods at prices higher than they paid for them.

This by no means suggests that you should love and admire all bankers, brokers, and other financial intermediaries. Some offer good deals and service; others decidedly not. Even if you enjoy a warm and mutually beneficial relationship with a banker or broker, there remains an adversarial element to that relationship. Since it is incumbent on you to know your adversary, it is necessary to be aware of commissions, fees, service charges—and spreads.

In the stock market, spreads can be difficult to determine. You cannot accompany your brokerage firm's representative down to the stock exchange floor to learn the specialist's bid (buying) and asked (selling) price. Even in cases where you may have access to published bid and asked quotations, as in the over-the-counter market, the figures may be outdated—even if they are only a few minutes old. They also may be only dealer-to-dealer figures that do not include a retail markup. In general, spreads tend to be narrowest in stocks that trade most actively, that have large numbers of shares in public hands, and that have financially strong or highly competitive market-makers. In a "thinly" traded, volatile stock, the spread tends to be wide.

There have been occasions when individual savers and investors have had the opportunity to beat some financial institutions at their own spread game. Suppose you had taken out an 8 percent mortgage at a savings and loan in 1975. About five years later, you could have purchased a time certificate of deposit from the same institution at an interest rate of 13, 14, or 15 percent, or even more. The only problem was, the situation presented a severe threat to the financial system on which the U.S. economy is based. Too bad, and quite possibly thank goodness, it didn't last.

STOP AND LIMIT ORDERS. The most usual way to enter an order with a brokerage firm is simply to request that the firm buy or sell stock for you "at the market"—for the best price it can get. It is not the only way, however. Among the other common types are stop and limit orders. Stop orders are normally used to protect against large losses. Limit orders may be used when you wish to specify a minimum price for which you are willing to sell, or a maximum price at which you are willing to buy.

Advocates of stop orders say they are a good means of following the time-honored precept "take your losses quickly; let your winners run." Suppose you buy a stock at 50. At the same time, you put in a standing order with your broker that it be sold immediately should the price go as low as 45. That night, you drop off to sleep peacefully, secure in the feeling that only 10 percent of your capital is at risk.

Well, not quite. The stop order does not guarantee that your stock will sell at 45. If some calamity befalls the company while you slumber, it may turn out that the stock opens the next day in the mid-30s. Anywhere at 45 or below, your stop order becomes a market order to sell, at whatever price a buyer is willing to pay.

If that prospect has you tossing and turning a bit, consider the possibility of a "whipsaw." From the moment you buy it at 50, the stock drifts lower, touching 44⅞ just long enough for your stop order to be executed. Then it zooms to 65. To stay flexible and try to avoid such mishaps, some investors employ what they call "mental stops," which they keep entered in their own minds rather than on any formal basis. Users of mental stops, of course, put heavy reliance on their own self-discipline.

As for limit orders, consider a case in which you have been following a stock that seems to be locked in a long-term trading range. Every time it reaches 20, it runs into selling pressure and drops back to about 15, where it seems to have a lot of friends. Here's a game you can play for fun and profit: Instruct your broker to buy every time it hits 15, and sell every time it reaches 20. The price you get or pay won't always be precise. Like a stop order, a limit order merely becomes a market order when the stock hits or passes the magic number. But with a strategy like this, how can you lose?

The answer to that is obvious. You can lose if the stock hits 15 on the way to 5. Or you can lose indirectly, but still painfully, if the stock passes 20 on the way to 50 and a two-for-one split. When you think a stock is attractive for fundamental reasons at $15 a share, many investment experts advise, don't niggle about paying $15.50 or $16 with a market order. If you think it's attractive only as a trading proposition, are you ready to bet you can consistently beat professional traders and market-makers, especially after you pay the commissions for each purchase and sale?

The options markets offer alternatives to stop and limit orders that any good broker should be able to explain. The catch is that these strategies always involve additional commission costs. To the degree that they protect you from risk, they also normally require that you sacrifice some potential gain.

SUMMER RALLY. Each year the arrival of warm weather on Wall Street seems to be accompanied by talk of when the traditional summer rally will occur and how strong it will be. Remember August 1982, brokers say, when a great bull market got off to a record-shattering start? Or how about the summer of '84, when the Dow Jones industrials jumped 87.46 points in a single week?

"For the past century or longer, members of the financial community have come to expect a healthy rally some time during the summer," says Yale Hirsch in his *Stock Trader's Almanac*. "But statistics show that a clearly identifiable summer rally does not occur with any reasonable consistency."

The story of the summer rally has been nurtured by a certain haziness of definition. If stock prices are generally falling, but stage a brief upward swing at some point in June, July, or August, does that qualify? If so, how much good does it do the typical investor? One common means of measuring the extent of the summer rally has been to compare the highest reading of the Dow between late June and the end of September with its low in May or June. But if you use that method, you are likely to come up with what looks like a meaningful advance in any year, except when stock prices fall steadily through the whole summer season.

"Such a big deal is made of the 'summer rally' that one might get the impression the market puts on its best razzle-dazzle performance in the summertime," Hirsch observes. "Nothing could be further from the truth. Not only does the market 'rally' in every season of the year, but it does so with more gusto in the winter, spring and fall than in the summer."

To arrive at that conclusion, Hirsch examined the behavior of the Dow Jones industrials going back to 1964. For the winter rally, he calculated the percentage gain from the low in November or December to the high in the first quarter. The spring rally was measured from the February–March low to the second quarter high, and so forth for the balance of the year.

The extremely positive bias of such a system is demonstrated by the fact that every quarter from the mid-1960s to the mid-1980s showed at least a modest gain. Severe bear markets like those of 1969–70 and 1973–74 magically disappear from the chart. What's more, Hirsch found, the winter "rallies" produced an average 11.7 percent gain; the autumn ones 10.3 percent; the spring ones 9.5 percent, and the summer ones 8.5 percent.

The precise origin of the Street's summer-rally tradition is buried in the murky past. It gained currency as a way for brokers to try to drum up business in the slowest season of the year, when many of their customers were too busy with vacations or other diversions to do much stock trading. Today, with investing institutions playing the dominant role in the marketplace, this seasonal slowdown in Wall Street's business is much less in evidence than it used to be. But the myth of the summer rally lives on.

SUPPORT AND RESISTANCE. Many students of the stock market seek to unravel the mysteries of the charts by looking for price levels at which individual stocks or the market as a whole have apparent support and resistance. To cite a simple example, suppose that Hypothetical Corp.'s stock in recent months has rallied each time it has fallen as low as about 24, but has stopped rising and turned back each time it reached 30. From this pattern emerges the conclusion that a significant number of investors consider the stock a good buy at about 24, but regard it as a sell candidate once it hits 30.

This way of thinking would seem to make sense. Just about any stock can be considered a good buy at the right price, and too expensive at some other given price level. Support may exist in the form of actual limit orders (discussed earlier) to buy Hypothetical, or simply in the form of a large body of investors who wish they had bought it at 24 and intend to do so if and when it gets that low again. Similarly with resistance—as well as the distinct possibility that there are a good many investors who bought the stock at around 30 some time back and are waiting for the chance to "get out even."

Chart-watchers have many ways of trying to spot presumed levels of support and resistance. They tend to look particularly for "breakouts," periods when stocks penetrate support and resistance levels, on the theory that they signal new potential gains or losses for those stocks. However, the fact that breakouts do occur illustrates one problem with support and resistance levels—assuming that they exist and can be spotted, no one can know for sure how long they will hold.

In early August of 1982, one investment adviser thought he had picked out a support level for the stock market at 780 in the Dow Jones industrial average. If the average went below that point, he figured, the market was due for a severe sell-off, and he told his subscribers so. Well, the average did go below 780 for four days, after which it embarked on one of its biggest advances in modern history.

There is a common tendency for commentators in the press

to describe round numbers in the Dow Jones industrial average as support or resistance levels. For many years, 1,000 seemed to be a formidable obstacle for the average to surmount. Some market-wise Wall Streeters derided all the talk about Dow 1,000, saying it had no significance. They might well have been right. But by the very nature of the market, if enough investors believed it was significant, then it might have become so.

One last commentary on the reliability of support and resistance levels: On Jan. 11, 1983, the Dow Jones industrials climbed to a new closing high of 1,051.70. That stood as the record for more than a decade, and lots of people on Wall Street presumed that it would act as a major stumbling block for the bull market that began in 1982. On Jan. 26, 1983, the Dow stood at 1,037.99. The next day, it jumped 25 points to 1,063. The supposed hurdle was cleared in a single day, and the average moved on to above 1,200 in the next three months.

TAX SELLING. In the closing stages of the year, the behavior of the stock market is often said to be distorted by selling for tax purposes. Brokers say this selling may be especially virulent in poor years for the market, since such years produce a large crop of losers that investors may want to unload before year-end to be able to write them off against their other earnings on their tax returns. Thus, stocks that are depressed in October may get more so in November and December without any apparent negative news affecting them.

In recent years, the effects of tax selling have probably diminished. More and more, the market is dominated by pension funds and other institutions that don't pay federal income taxes, and that therefore are rarely or never motivated by tax considerations in their buying and selling decisions. Nevertheless, followers of the stock market say there are a couple of important points to bear in mind on the subject of tax selling.

The first is to act early if you plan to do some tax selling of your own. If you own stock that is a candidate for year-end dumping for tax purposes, it makes sense to sell it before everybody else with the same thing in mind gets around to doing so, pushing the price relentlessly downward. Something in human nature seems to encourage procrastination in matters of taxes and tax planning—a tendency on which an alert investor may be able to capitalize.

Secondly, many financial advisers say venturesome investors may seek to take advantage of tax selling by shopping for "bargains" among depressed issues near the end of the year. In theory, the price of a stock that is getting pounded by tax selling may be artificially low, in the sense that tax selling is going to stop once the new year arrives. Of course, any trading strategy based on this premise will work out best if the market happens to have a roaring rally as the new year begins. If it should turn out that the market takes a dive, your tax-sale bargains may "outperform" the averages and still leave you with a loss.

TECHNICAL ANALYSIS. What more enduring image of Wall Street and its mystique than the technical analyst with his (and increasingly these days, her) charts, indicators and arcane vocabulary? Amid all the talk of moving averages, head-and-shoulders tops, and put-call ratios, technical analysts set themselves a relatively straightforward mission: to try to divine something of the stock market's future through the study of its past and present behavior.

Technicians have long been derided by Wall Streeters in the fundamental analysis camp, in much the same way that an astronomer would speak of an astrologer. The name at one time carried such dubious honor that it prompted Robert Stovall, a well-known Wall Street commentator, to remark, "Please—we prefer to be known as 'market historians.' "

Yet as many of its practitioners would insist, technical analysis is not so illogical. It is an attempt to measure the two forces that determine stock prices, supply and demand. Years ago one Wall Street analyst, Leslie Pollack, drew an analogy with decision-making in a manufacturing business. The management of a manufacturing company monitors orders, and opts to produce the merchandise that is selling the best, rather than that which it thinks is the most aesthetically appealing. In taking this pragmatic approach, Pollack said, it is in effect opting for technical analysis rather than fundamental analysis.

Today almost every major brokerage firm has at least one resident technician. To keep the blue-chip clientele happy, he or she may be referred to as a "market strategist," "director of the market analysis group," or something similar. Respectable or not, of course, technical analysis has yet to find any magic keys to unlock the secret of what the stock market will do in the future. Like many other followers of the stock market, you may find it fascinating, even profitable. By the same token, it may be of relatively little interest to you if you are following a long-term strategy of accumulating stocks regardless of market conditions prevailing in any given day, or week, or month.

TOTAL RETURN. Some investors venture into the stock market with capital gains (quite often big capital gains) in mind. Others buy high-yielding stocks in quest of income. The choices they make are based on how much risk they want to take and their tax circumstances, among other factors. Indeed, no two investors are in precisely identical situations, with precisely identical goals. But in their preoccupation with all these very real concerns, people sometimes forget that the central point of the whole exercise of investing is to make money. If, through a combination of dividends and capital gains, you can earn, say, a 15 percent annual return after taxes and commissions with a given stock, you may naturally consider yourself a winner.

The relatively simple concept of total return has drawn renewed attention in recent years with the rise to prominence of tax-exempt investors such as pension funds. Since market participants like these don't have to worry about the tax consequences, they care little whether their return comes in the form of dividends or capital gains—as long as that return is a good

one. Many individual investors also practice total-return investing in their individual retirement accounts, Keogh plans, or other
vehicles that don't incur any tax obligation.

In direct investing, however, it should be remembered that
your total return might not be the same as someone else's if it
incurs a big tax bill or doesn't serve your short- and long-term
needs. Capital gains earned on risky investments may be a welcome addition to the nest egg of a retiree trying to live on a
stable, limited budget. But the strategy that brought in those
capital gains might have been totally inappropriate for that individual. In the ideal, the retiree puts his or her money in an
investment that provides the desired degree of safety and yield.
If something unexpected happens to cause the value of the investment to increase as well, then the investor is entitled to a
little gloating over the total return achieved.

UNDERVALUED-OVERVALUED. These terms are common
descriptives on Wall Street for securities that someone considers
a bargain (undervalued) or a bad buy (overvalued). No matter
how the conclusion is arrived at, these judgments are always
subjective, since the only true value a stock or other security has
is the highest price someone is willing to pay for it at any given
time. You may hear, for example, that a stock is selling at less
than its value should the company be liquidated, or that its real
estate (or oil reserves, or whatever) alone is worth more than
what the stock is currently selling for. To many investors, including some of the most successful and respected, the search
for undiscovered value is what stock-market investing is all about.

Of course, it should always be borne in mind that today's
hidden values can remain unrecognized by the market for an in-
definite period of time in the future. If there is no likely prospect that a company is going to be liquidated, and if that same
company has a lot of operating problems, the theoretical liquidating value of its stock may not mean much. Conversely, stocks
that seem overvalued at price-earnings ratios of 25 to 1 have been
known to rise to PEs of 30 or 35 or 40. When you are con-

fronted with someone talking up an "undervalued situation," you might inquire what is likely to happen in the reasonable future to cause the market to recognize that purported value.

VENTURE CAPITAL. Venture capitalists are sophisticated investors who put up money for fledgling businesses, almost always through private transactions. They tend to be well-heeled enough to diversify their money, so that only a few of their high-risk investments need to pay off for them to achieve handsome rewards. In the period before many a company attains sufficient status to sell stock to the public, it finances its operations and development with venture capital.

This is a point to bear in mind when you are offered the chance to "get in on the ground floor" with a hot new issue. As you consider the price of the public offering, you might ask yourself how much early venture-capital investors paid for their shares. Of course, the venture capitalists may well have taken risks you would have been unwilling to bear. The stock at its public offering price may well be an attractive proposition. But as for "getting in on the ground floor," that's saying a bit much if private investors already have had a big, profitable ride from the same company.

WINDOW-DRESSING. This is a practice widely ascribed on Wall Street to mutual funds and other money-management operations that report not only their performance results, but a list of their actual holdings, to shareholders or clients periodically—say, every quarter. Suppose that in May a given stock or other investment takes a big drop amid much fanfare. By the end of June, it stands to reason, fund managers who had held a lot of the stock might well want to clean it out of their portfolios to avoid the embarrassment of listing a big loser in their midyear reports. Similarly, they might feel the temptation to load up on recent big winners as the quarter nears an end.

Window-dressing is occasionally used by market commentators as an explanation for fluctuations in stock prices in the last few trading sessions of a quarter. There are no statistics available to show how much of this type of activity actually takes place. It may well be that its significance and impact are generally exaggerated. Nevertheless, if you are considering buying a depressed stock in early March, for example, you might consider waiting until later in the month to see if you can get it for a lower price as disenchanted investors dump it before the end of the quarter.

For mutual fund investors, there does not seem to be any reason for great concern about window-dressing—unless you have some cause to suspect that the fund management is devoting a lot of time, effort and expense to this kind of thing while neglecting its basic mission. The fund's net asset value is available for your constant and convenient inspection in the newspaper, and there is no way any fund can window-dress its net asset value, short of blatant, and unlikely, fraud.

YIELD CURVE. In order to compare yields available on different types of interest-bearing investments, many Wall Street analysts plot what they call yield curves. The investments involved may be similar ones of varying maturities—for instance, one-year Treasury bills, five-year Treasury notes, and 30-year Treasury bonds. Or they may be similar ones of varying quality—for instance, typical municipal bonds rated triple-A, double-A, and single-A.

Normally, but not always, yields of investments with long maturities tend to be higher than comparable ones with shorter maturities, since the former require a commitment of your money for a longer period of time. Normally, yields of lower-quality investments tend to be higher than those of their better-quality relatives because of the difference in risk involved. One purpose of looking at the yield curve is to determine whether longer-maturity or lower-quality securities offer enough potential extra reward to justify buying them.

Consider a case in which one-year Treasury bills are yielding 7.5 percent; five-year Treasury notes 9.8 percent, and 30-

year Treasury bonds 10.2 percent. From one to five years, the yield curve is relatively steep, but after that it flattens out. An investment adviser might in these circumstances suggest that the five-year notes are the most attractive proposition.

With some practice, the 15-Minute Investor does not need a computer, or even a pencil and graph paper, to plot the yield curve. A glance at the yields as shown in your daily newspaper, or at those quoted by a bond dealer, will enable you to visualize it in your mind.

Even if you are not a candidate to invest in fixed-income securities, a periodic check on the yield curve can serve as something of a guide to prevailing sentiment among investors. An extremely steep yield curve, for example, suggests that the large population of investors in the government securities market are confident about the near-term outlook for interest rates and inflation, but not so comfortable with longer-term prospects. Strange aberrations in yield curves may sometimes be symptoms of unsettled times on Wall Street.

INDEX